SHANKS & SHIVS

Prison Knives

ERIC "SUPERMAN" STURGESS

Rose Of Sharon
PUBLISHING

ERIC "SUPERMAN" STURGESS

Printed Worldwide
First Printing 2024
First Edition 2024
10 9 8 7 6 5 4 3 2 1
Rose of Sharon Publishing books may be ordered through booksellers or by contacting:
Rose Of Sharon Publishing roseofsharonpublishing.com
P.O. Box 186
Floresville, Texas 78114

ISBN: 978-1-962743-88-4 Paperback

SHANKS & SHIVS
Prison Knives

Dedication

I dedicate this book to all the people who did not have a positive, strong, and moral male role model while growing up. Most men in prison came from fatherless homes, or if the dad was around, he was a horrible role model. Absentee fathers are causing society to pay a high price for their low living and lack of leadership.

By the Grace of God, I have given my children everything I never had as a child. God bless the men who take their responsibility as fathers seriously and are positively involved in their children's lives. More than ever, we need strong and moral men to lead their families boldly and set an example of how to live.

"When my mother and father forsake me, then the Lord will take care of me,"
Psalm 27:10.

Table of Contents

Introduction

A banger is an inmate-manufactured weapon made out of steel meticulously cut away from a larger piece of metal. Inmates manufacture bangers out of various items that can be found on a prison compound. A piece of metal from a chain link fence then straightened, makes a righteous ice pick. Food carts, bunks, desks, and lockers are everyday items that pieces of metal are cut from by inmates to make a banger. Bangers are also constructed from plastic melted together and then sharpened. These makeshift plastic weapons in the hands of a hardened convict are as lethal as any knife built out of prison steel.

Years ago, inmates using dental floss coated in powdered toothpaste or Ajax cleaners cut steel from objects. Dental floss covered in powdered toothpaste can slowly cut through a steel bar over time, which inmates have copious amounts of. The hardened blade from a pair of nail or hair clippers is also used to gradually cut away steel from various objects to make weapon stock. The easiest and most common way for inmates to cut away pieces of metal in prison is by using a hacksaw blade.

To conceal the missing piece of metal, inmates make a paste from numerous substances, then cover the hole and paint it so officers will not notice. Some prisons have officers use rubber mallets when inspecting a cell, so these false voids are discovered when they hit it. Some bangers are constructed out of material that isn't sturdy and only good for one stabbing. In prison, these bangers are called a one hitta quitta because they usually break after poking someone. Sometimes, bangers will be made with a short blade because they aren't trying to kill a person; they will blast one of their homies as punishment for violating their household policies. This stabbing against one of their members with a short banger is called a soft move juxtaposed with a hard move. A hard move is when they try to take the wind of their intended victim and murder them.

Some bangers will have a looped shoestring or other material added to the hilt so that it can be wrapped around the wrist of the attacker. This is done so the weapon cannot be grabbed or knocked out of their hand while poking their victim. I have heard about inmates who used tape to fasten a knife to their hands before they attacked someone.

A bone crusher is a huge knife made out of prison steel that was given its name because it will usually break bones when you are blasted with it. The average prison banger is like a pocketknife, while a bone crusher is like a Bowie knife. Getting moved on with a bone crusher usually results in severe injuries.

A tomahawk is a razor melted onto a toothbrush, used in a slashing motion to inflict horrific injuries on the victim's face and neck. I have talked with various officers on many occasions, and every single one of us agreed a tomahawk was the weapon we feared most to get attacked with. All officers admitted they would rather be poked with a banger than sliced with a tomahawk because its injuries are devastating compared to an average inmate-manufactured weapon.

Some inmates can be seen with a very long scar along their faces, resulting from being sliced with a tomahawk. That scar is often called the mark of shame or puto mark because snitches, chomos, people who don't pay their debts, and gang dropouts get sliced in their faces in that manner. Wherever they go in the prison system after that, everybody will know they are no good because of the noticeable scar on their face. The mark of shame usually starts at the corner of the lip and moves upward towards the ear and neck area. It often takes hundreds of stitches to close those ghastly wounds a tomahawk makes.

While working in Administration Segregation, one of my road dogs at Centinela State Prison was sliced in his face with a tomahawk. It took over 150 stitches and many surgeries to fix the vast and grotesque wound on his face. An inmate was in the shower, and he purposely dropped something outside the locked grill gate and asked him to pick it up. When my friend bent over in front of the shower, the inmate reached out of the handcuff port and viciously sliced him across the face. Inmates were not allowed razors in the hole for this very reason. However, some of them still managed to have them in their possession despite our best efforts to restrict their access to them.

Weapon stock is a term used in prison to describe metal or plastic that has been cut and even sharpened, but a handle hasn't been attached yet, so the banger isn't ready for use yet. Weapon stock is material one step away from being used to poke someone in prison. Melted plastic is a prevalent item used for a handle on a banger in prison. T-shirts, sheets, socks, and pillowcases are also used as handles for a knife.

Convicts routinely transport knives in prison by hooping them in their anal cavities. In order to insert the banger into their anus more quickly, the convicts will grease the tracks with various types of lubricants. Bangers will have a protective layer placed over them, such as toilet paper and then cellophane, before they are placed in the rectum so that it will not cause serious injury. After a banger has been in the anal cavity for several hours, it tends to get covered in fecal matter. Due to this effect, getting blasted in prison got the nickname of hard candy because the knife wrapped in cellophane pulled from the rectum looked like a candy bar. I have heard some convicts joke they can sometimes smell when somebody is about to get stabbed because of the odor of feces on the knife in the local vicinity. I also heard a story about a convict who had poop all over his mustache after biting the protective coating off of the banger he just pulled from his prison safe.

Convicts will practice dropping a banger out of their anal cavity for hours until they can do it in seconds. At first, a fish inmate will struggle to do this, but in time, they all learn to be proficient in dropping a banger from inside their rectum. Usually, a banger inserted into the rectum will have a little string attached to the handle called a rat tail, making it easier to get out. The rat tail will hang outside the rectum so the inmate can quickly grab it and pull the knife out.

An inmate nicknamed Spanky described how they would hoop their bangers: "When we had weapons, and the police were doing searches, we would wrap it up in plastic and take it to the hoop. You have to watch how you sit and move to avoid getting poked. All of the homies do it. If they have a weapon, it's going up there."

Convicts sometimes dip their bangers in blood and feces before they move on somebody to help promote infection in the wound caused by the weapon. This poor man's chemical warfare is called adding poison to your banger, and it is an ingenious way to inflict more damage on your enemy. When it comes to war in the penitentiary, convicts are creative in their tactics and devious in their methods.

Most gangs have a no-hands policy on level IV prison yards in California. This means gang members cannot fight each other with fists. If they can't resolve their issue, they can grab a banger, go into a cell, and stab it out until one man is left standing. Gangs need all their soldiers on Level IV yards; they don't want to lose them to Administrative Segregation for petty fights. If a gang lost soldiers to inconsequential fistfights among its members, they would become easier targets for other gangs, hence the no-hands policy.

Most factions have an area of the prison yard where they store the bangers; some refer to it as a steel garden. Bangers buried in the steel garden might have a clump of grass or weeds on top of them to mark their location. They might bury a banger ten steps from a noticeable landmark on the yard. For example, ten steps from the northern corner of their bench on the yard is a banger buried in the ground. Some factions in prison have specific people responsible for keeping track of all weapons and their locations on the yard. Prison gangs are very organized and keep track of everything, similar to any army in a war zone. Most factions in prison will have schooling for fish inmates to train them on making weapons. This instruction will usually have the fish make a banger, and then they will grade it. If it wasn't made properly, they will have them do it again until it is satisfactory.

They will also teach them how to make a fire to melt plastic to make a banger if they can't get their hands on any metal.

Many correctional officers tend to collect contraband made by inmates, and prison-made bangers are at the top of the list, closely followed by tattoo rigs. Correctional officers search the prison yards semi-regularly with metal detectors to find weapons buried in the grass and dirt. If you are alone or with your trusted partner, you might pocket some prison-made knives to take home and add to your vast collection. One of my road dogs had a trunk full of bangers from his many years at Centinela State Prison. Several officers at Centinela had dozens of bangers in their collections they had discovered over the years.

Shanks & Shivs

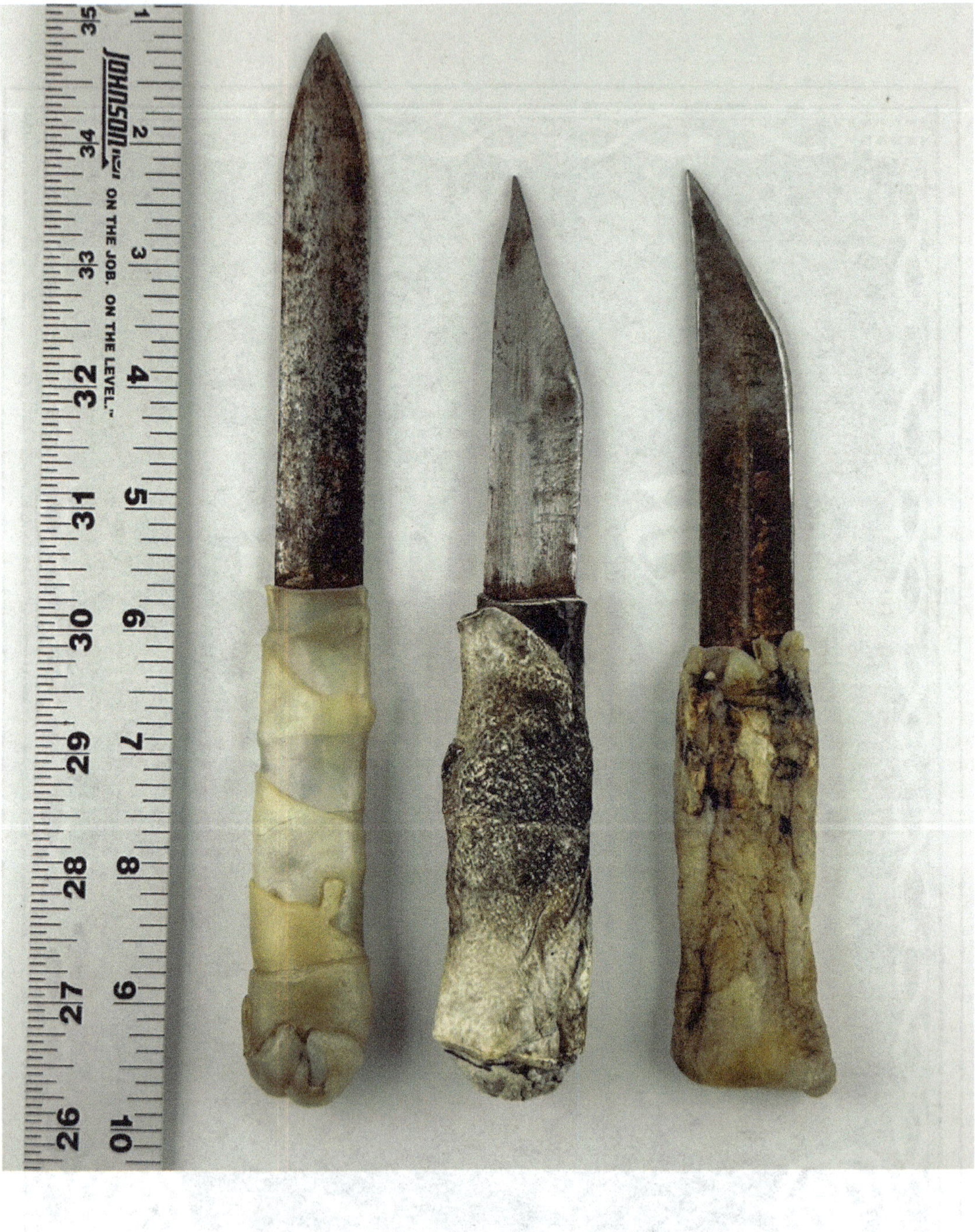
JOHNSON
ON THE JOB. ON THE LEVEL.

JOHNSON
ON THE JOB. ON THE LEVEL.™

JOHNSON
ON THE JOB. ON THE LEVEL.™

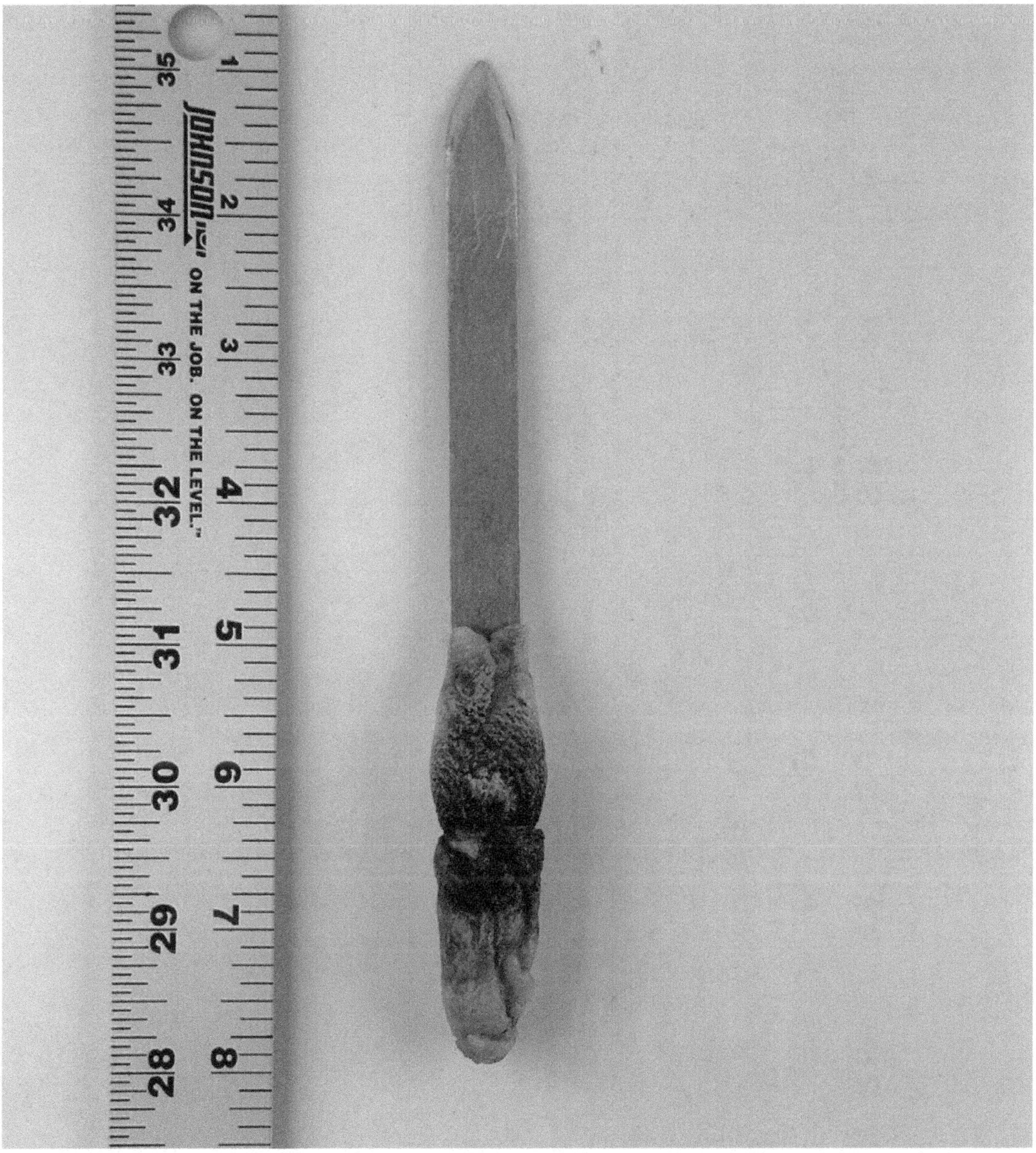
JOHNSON
ON THE JOB. ON THE LEVEL.™

JOHNSON
“ON THE JOB. ON THE LEVEL.”

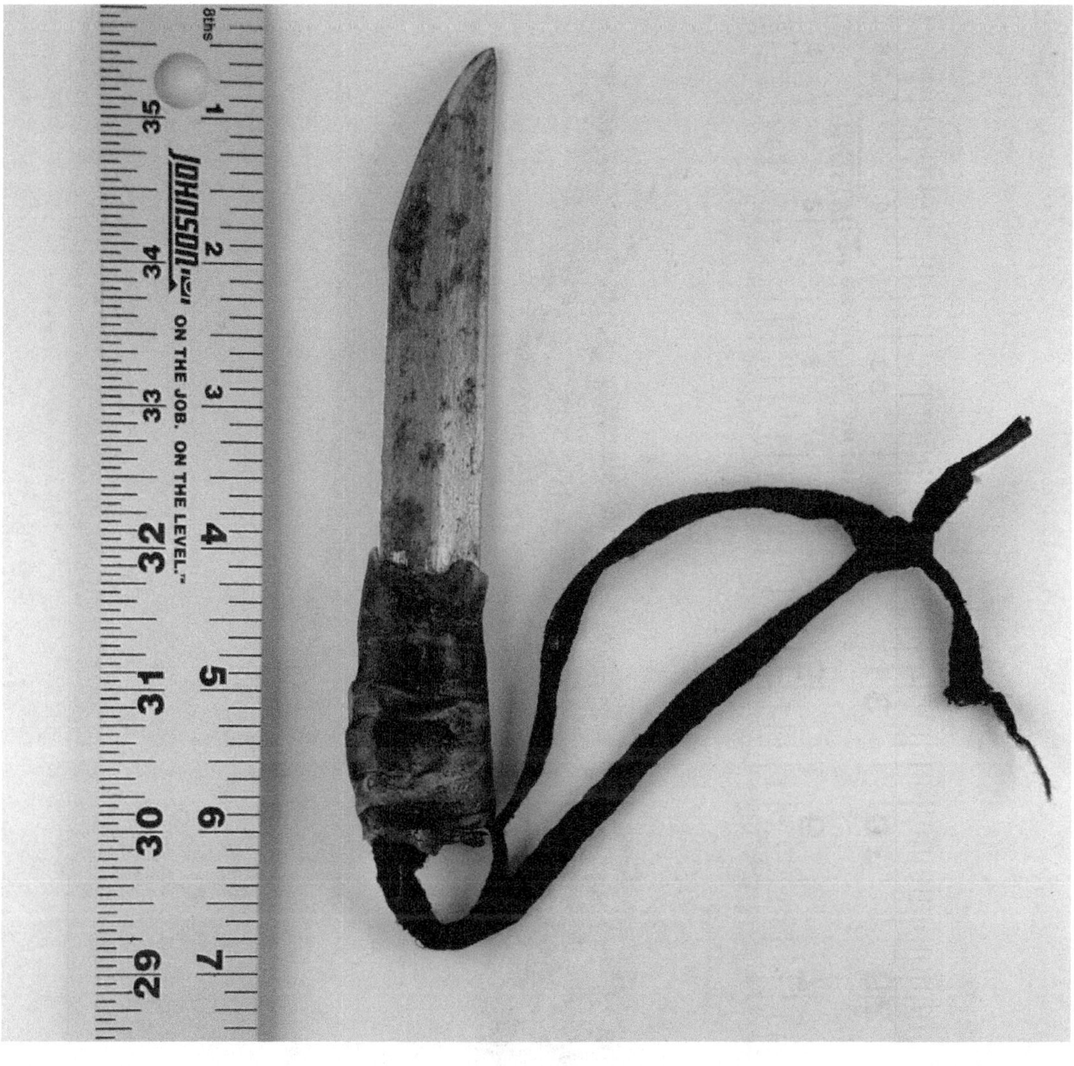
JOHNSON
ON THE JOB. ON THE LEVEL.™

JOHNSON
"ON THE JOB. ON THE LEVEL."

JOHNSON
ON THE JOB. ON THE LEVEL.™

JOHNSON ON THE JOB. ON THE LEVEL.™

JOHNSON
ON THE JOB. ON THE LEVEL.

JOHNSON
"ON THE JOB. ON THE LEVEL."

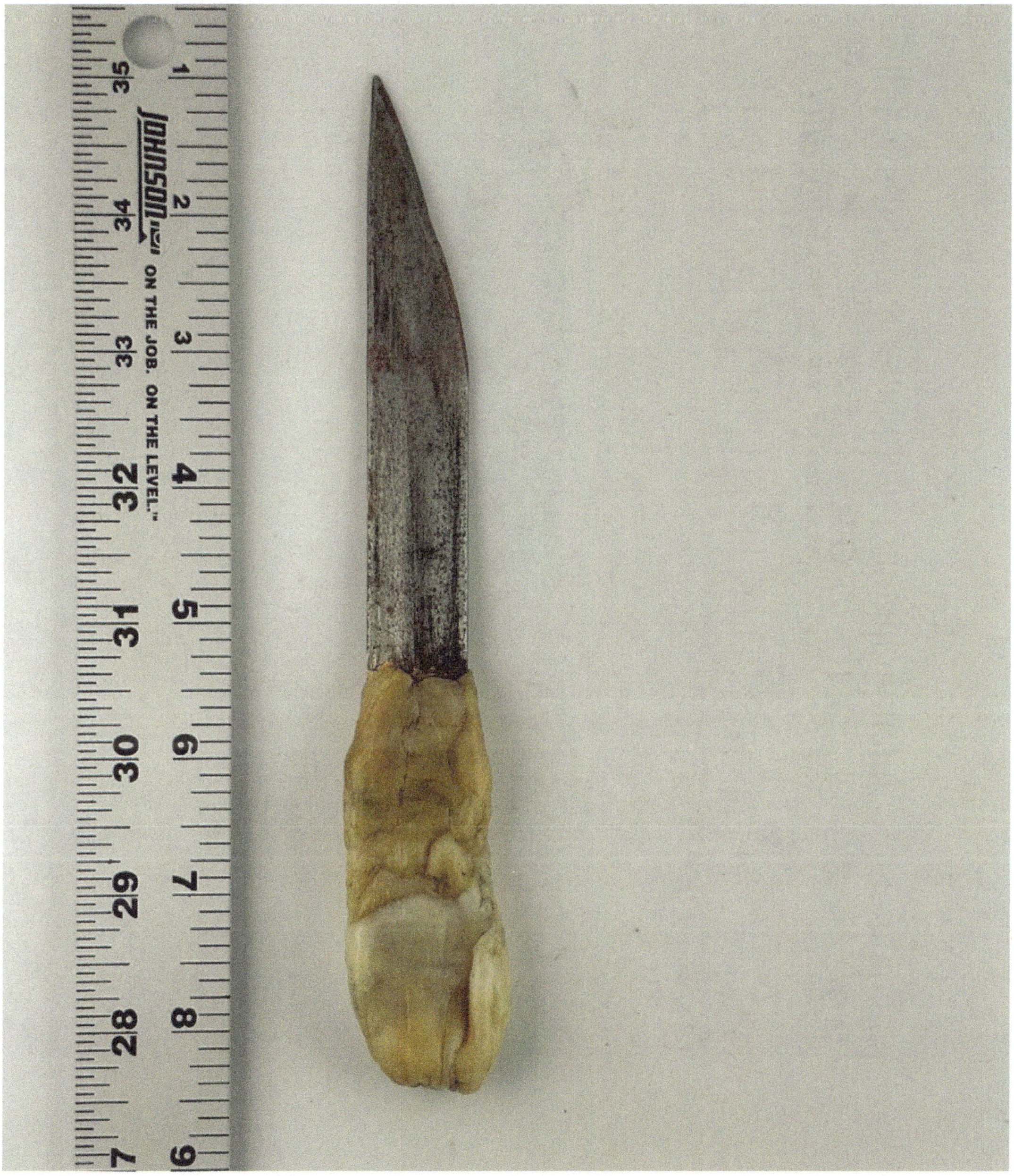
JOHNSON
"ON THE JOB. ON THE LEVEL."

JOHNSON
ON THE JOB. ON THE LEVEL.™

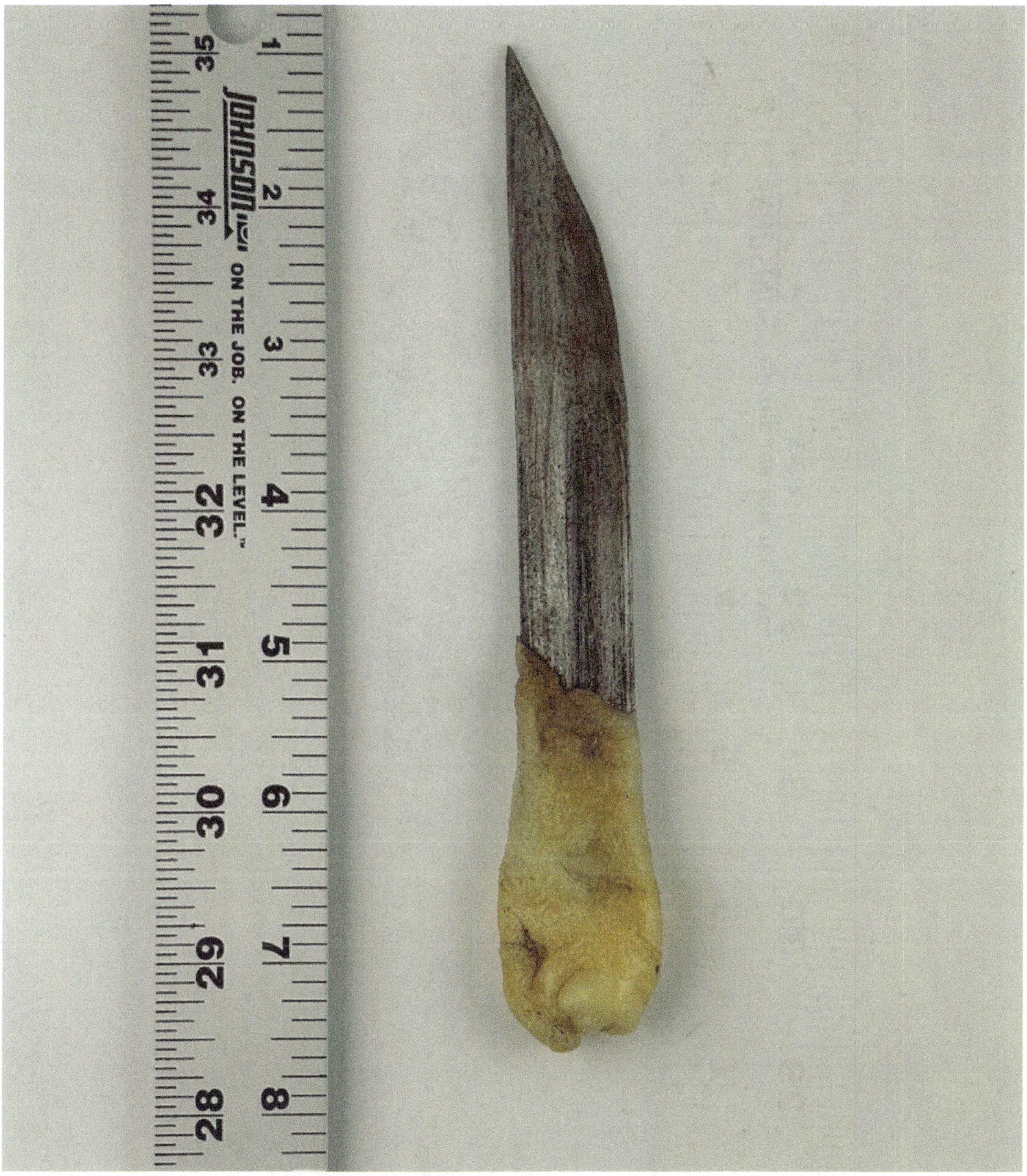
JOHNSON
ON THE JOB. ON THE LEVEL.™

8ths
JOHNSON
ON THE JOB. ON THE LEVEL.™

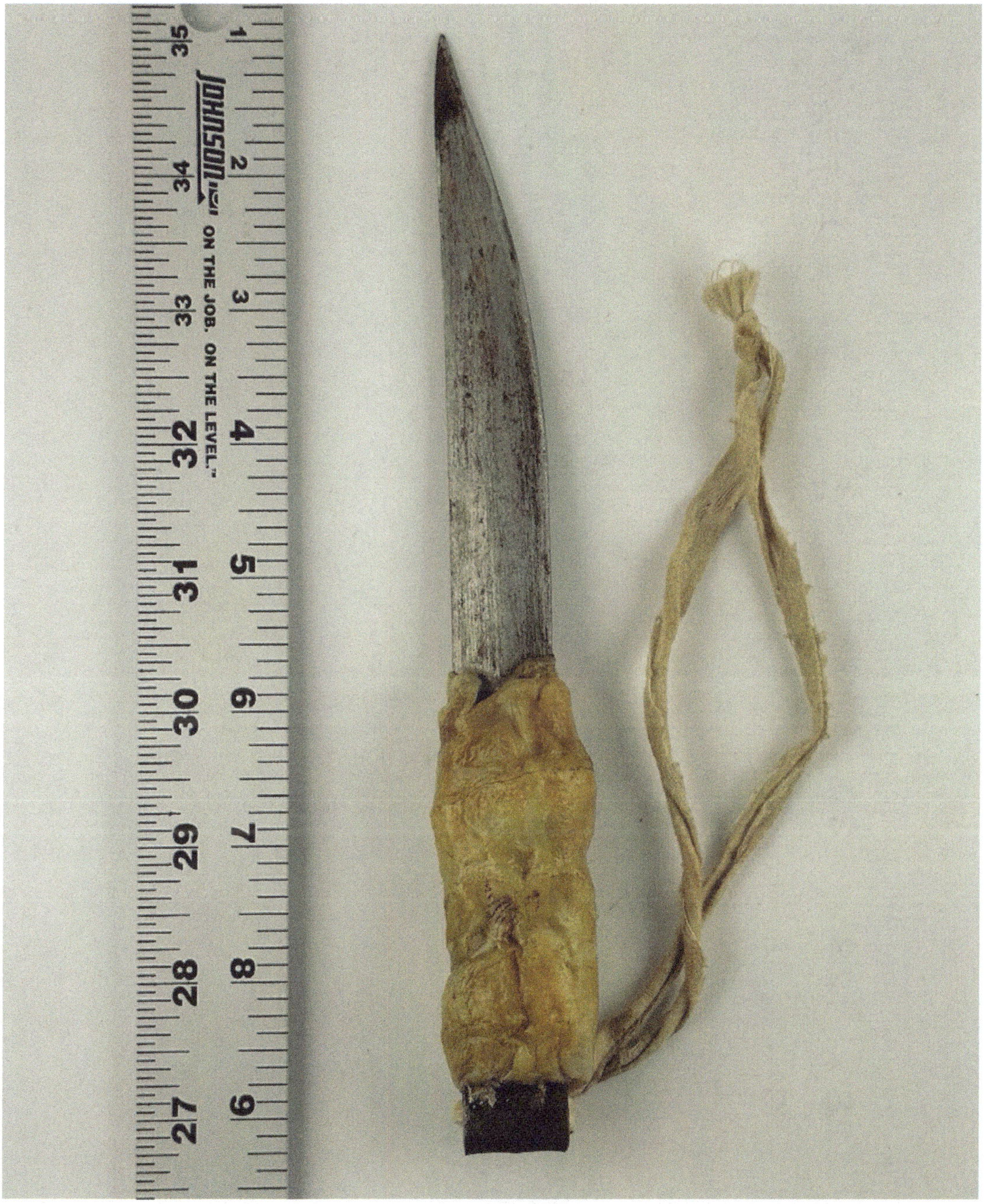
JOHNSON
"ON THE JOB. ON THE LEVEL."

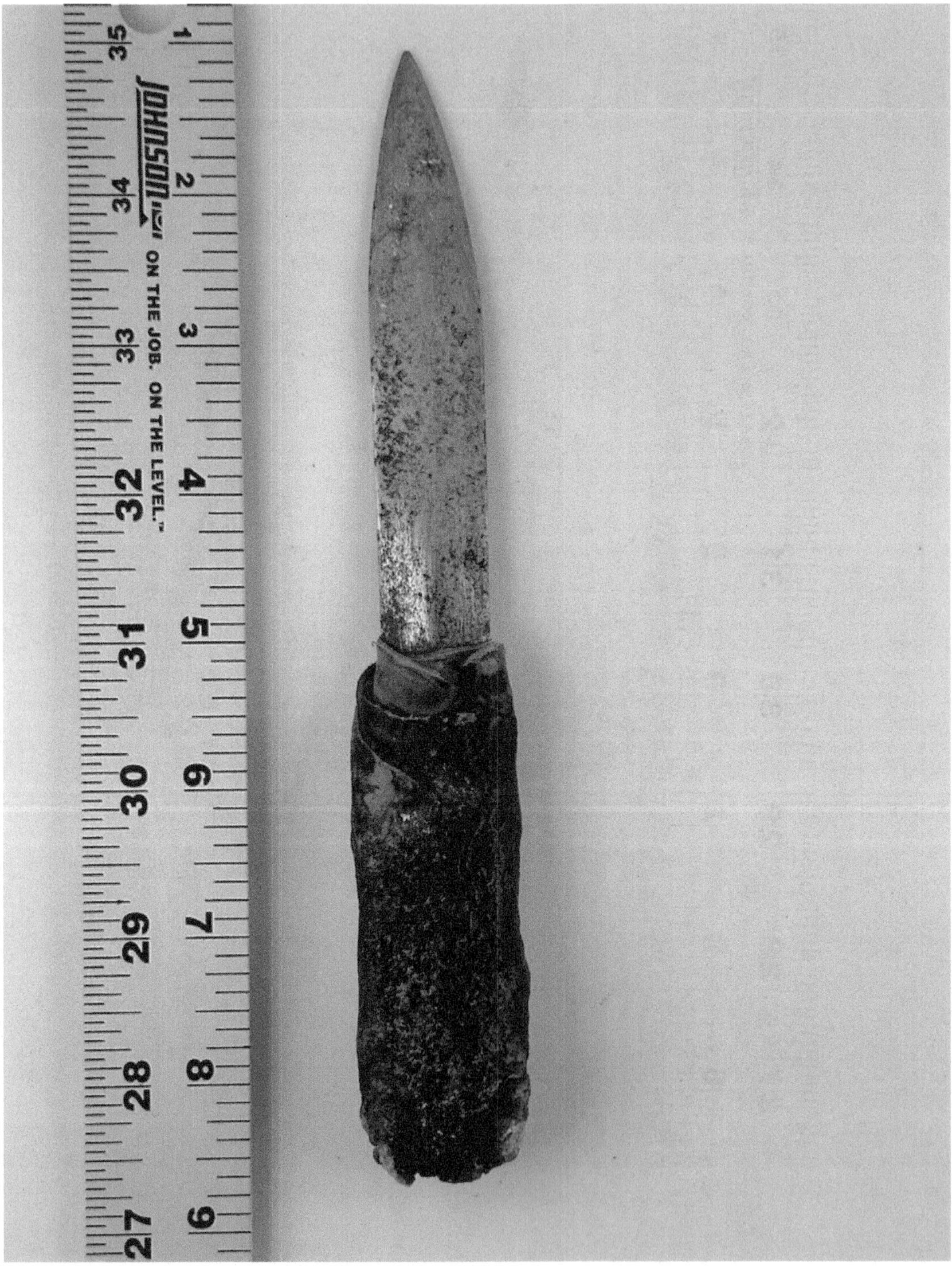
JOHNSON
ON THE JOB. ON THE LEVEL.™

JOHNSON
ON THE JOB. ON THE LEVEL.

JOHNSON
"ON THE JOB. ON THE LEVEL."

JOHNSON
ON THE JOB. ON THE LEVEL.™

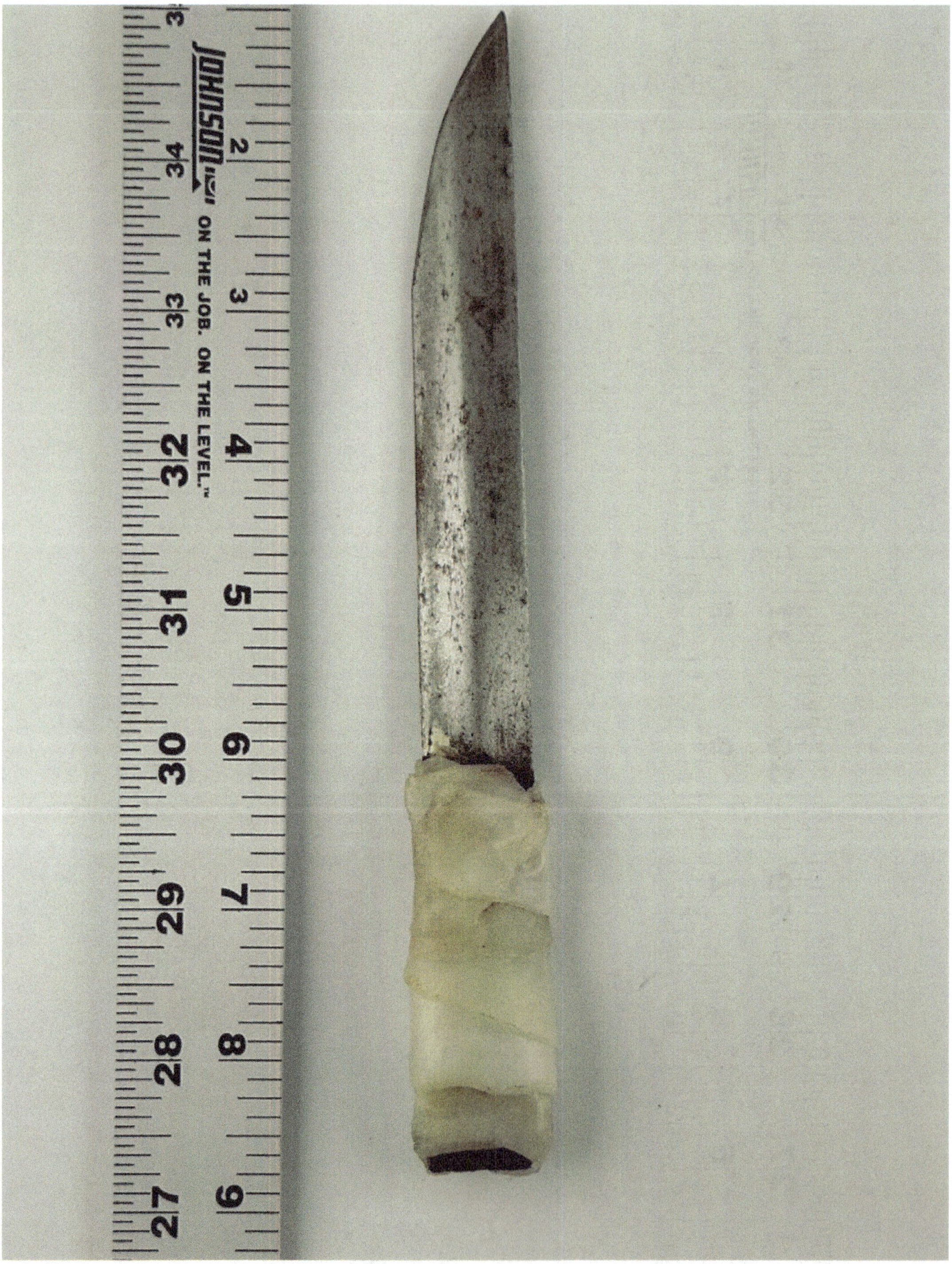
JOHNSON
ON THE JOB. ON THE LEVEL.™

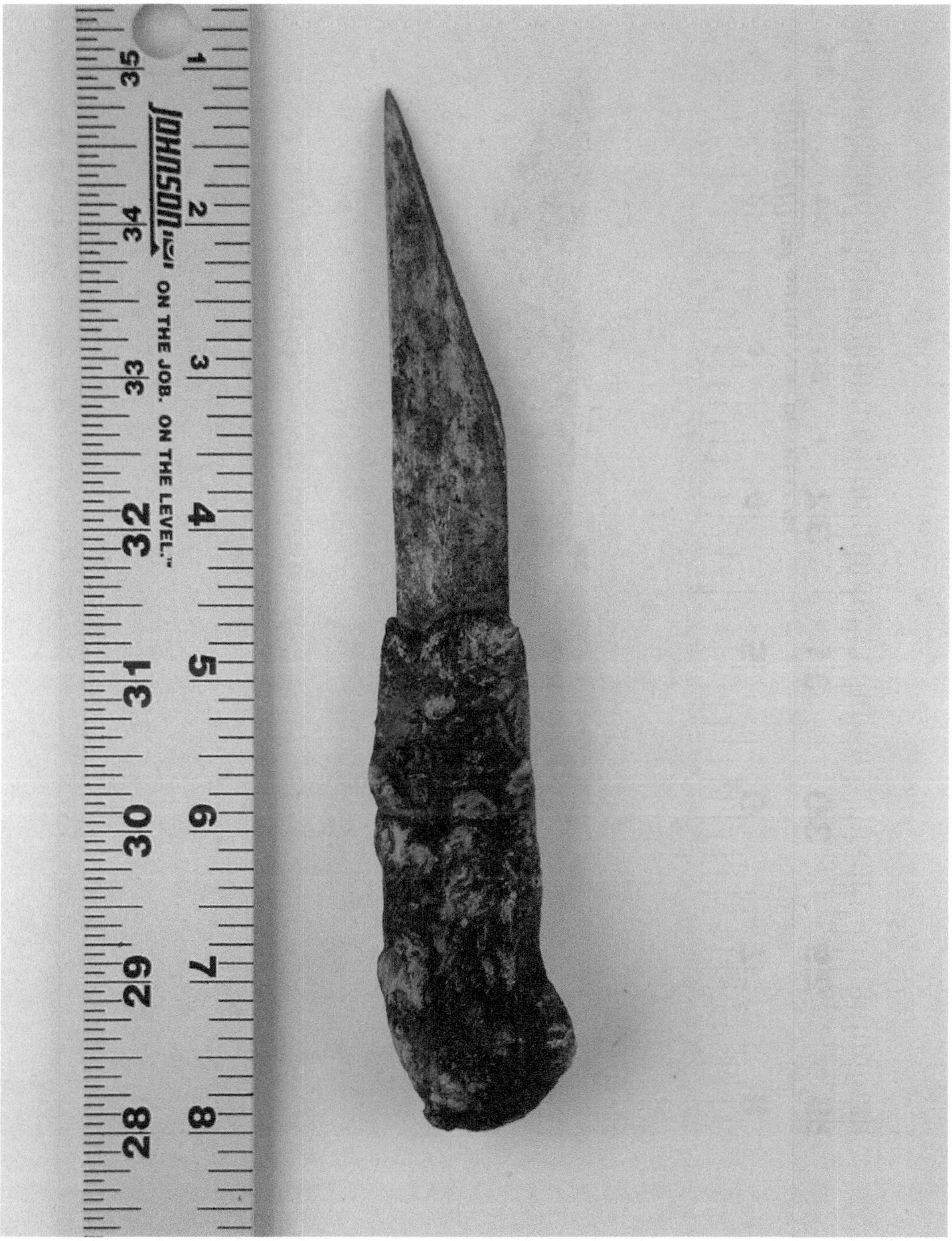
JOHNSON
ON THE JOB. ON THE LEVEL.™

JOHNSON
ON THE JOB. ON THE LEVEL.™

JOHNSON
ON THE JOB. ON THE LEVEL.™

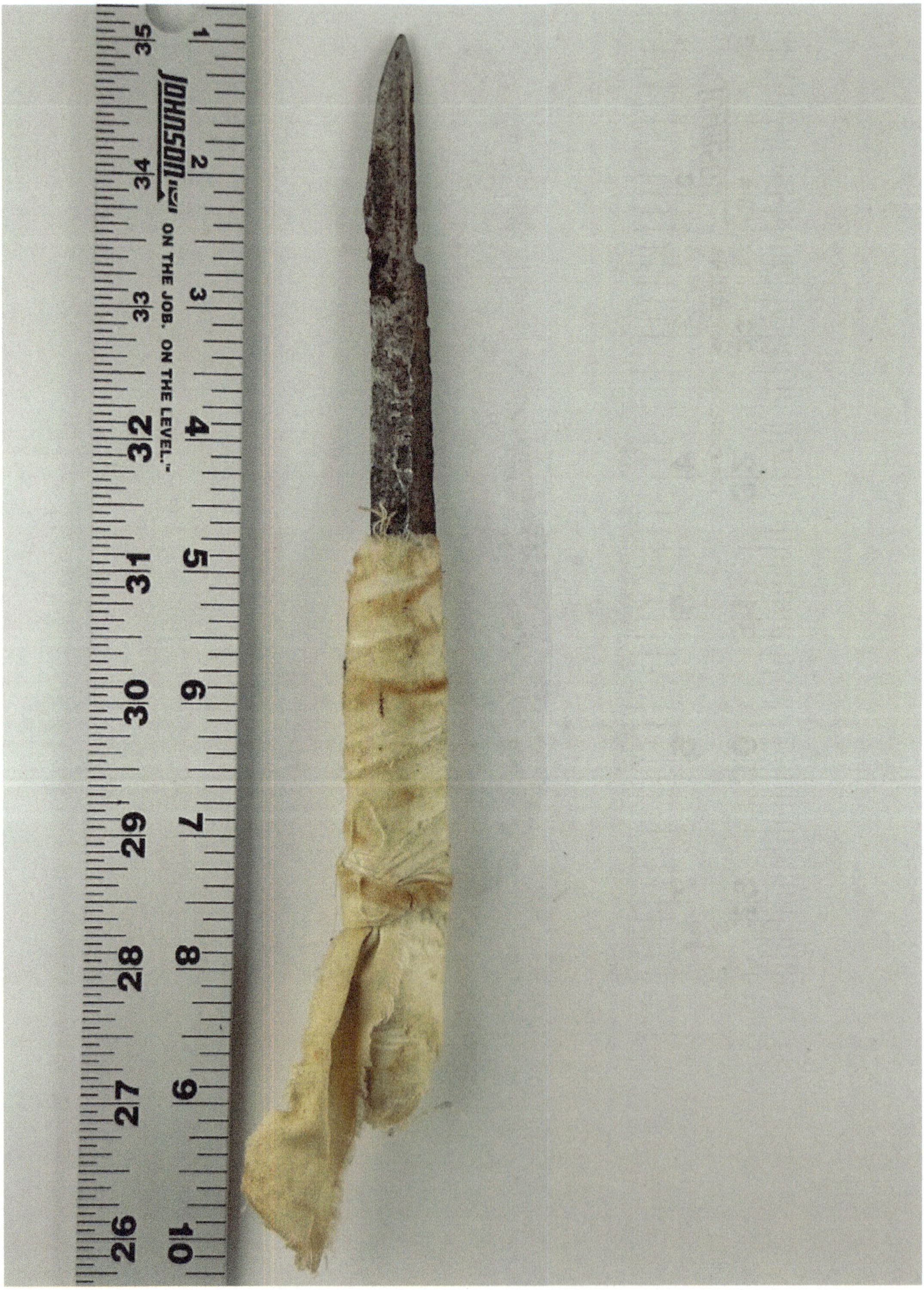
JOHNSON
ON THE JOB. ON THE LEVEL."

JOHNSON
ON THE JOB. ON THE LEVEL.™

JOHNSON
ON THE JOB. ON THE LEVEL.™

JOHNSON
ON THE JOB. ON THE LEVEL.

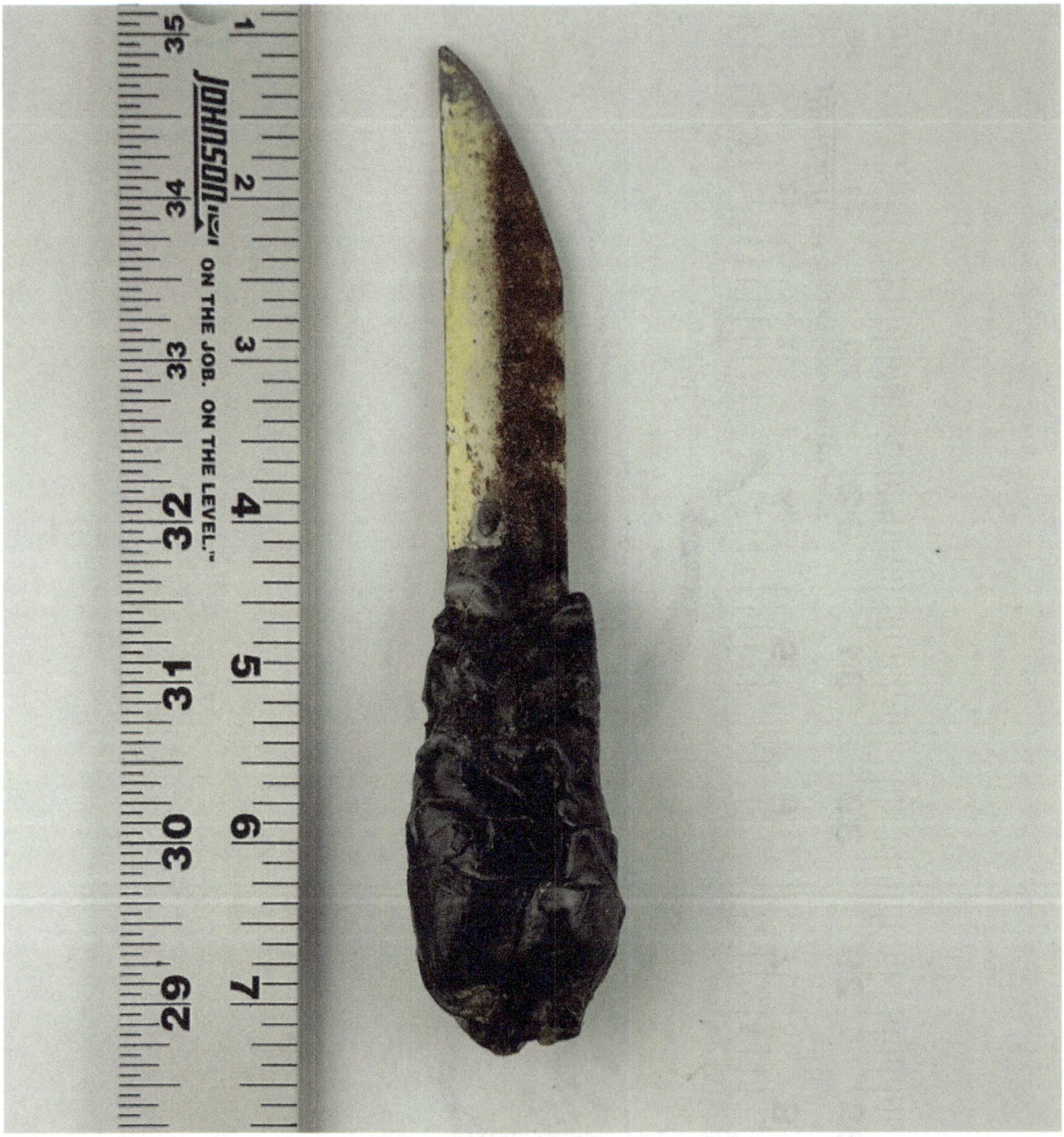
JOHNSON
ON THE JOB. ON THE LEVEL."

JOHNSON
ON THE JOB. ON THE LEVEL.

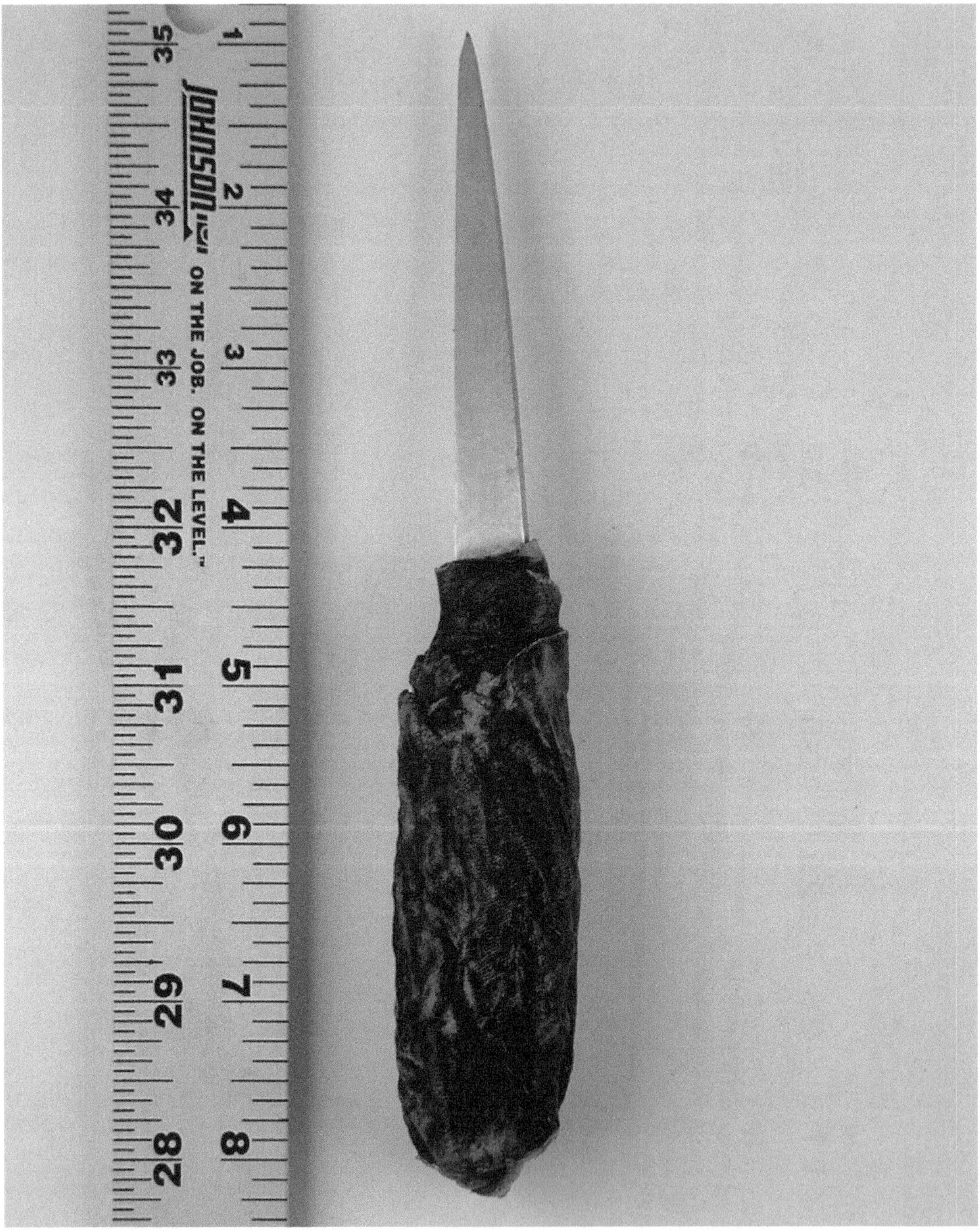
JOHNSON
ON THE JOB. ON THE LEVEL.™

JOHNSON
ON THE JOB. ON THE LEVEL.™

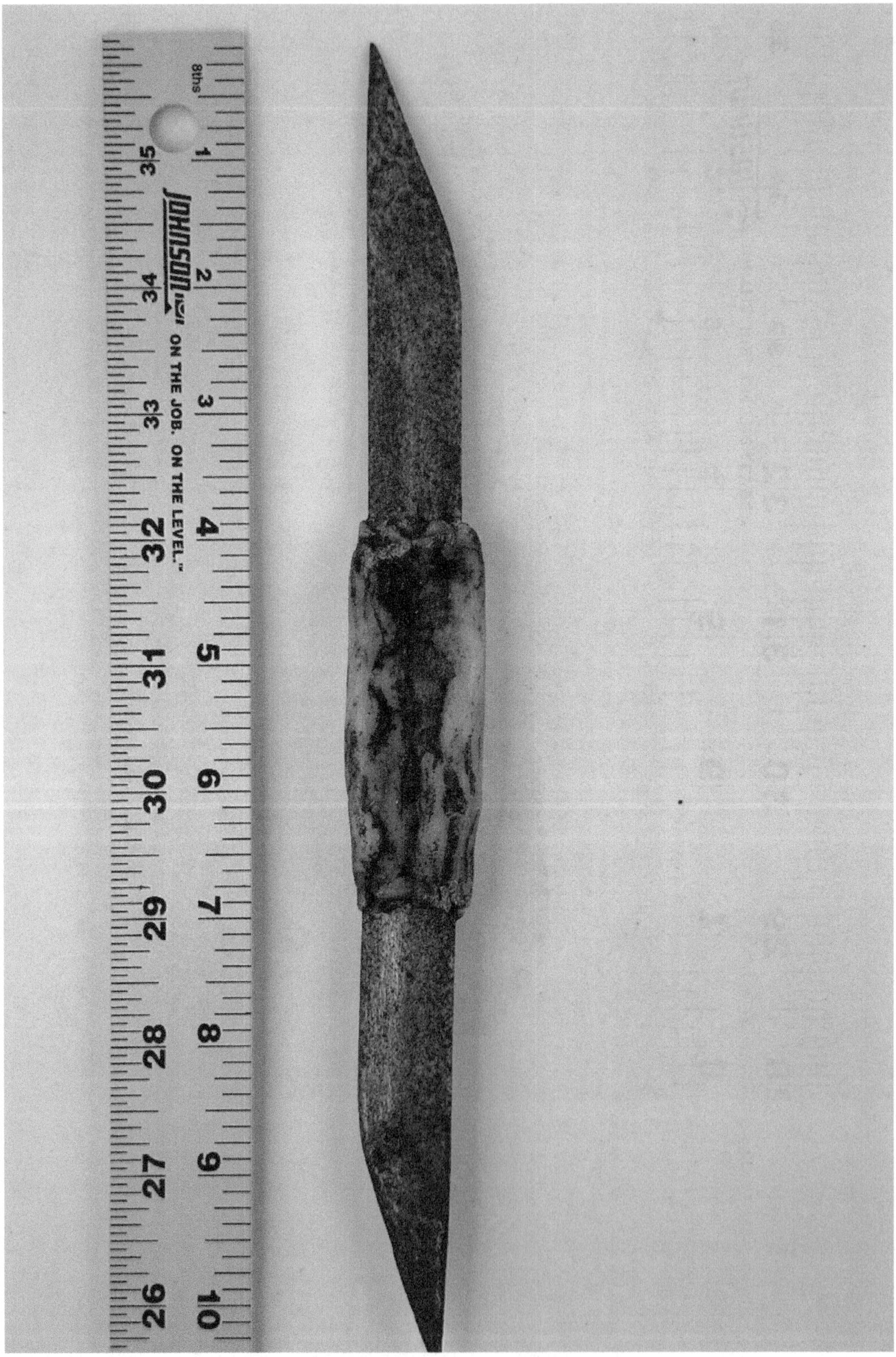
JOHNSON
"ON THE JOB. ON THE LEVEL."

JOHNSON
ON THE JOB. ON THE LEVEL.™

JOHNSON
ON THE JOB. ON THE LEVEL.™

JOHNSON
ON THE JOB. ON THE LEVEL.™

JOHNSON
"ON THE JOB. ON THE LEVEL."

JOHNSON
"ON THE JOB. ON THE LEVEL."

JOHNSON
"ON THE JOB. ON THE LEVEL."

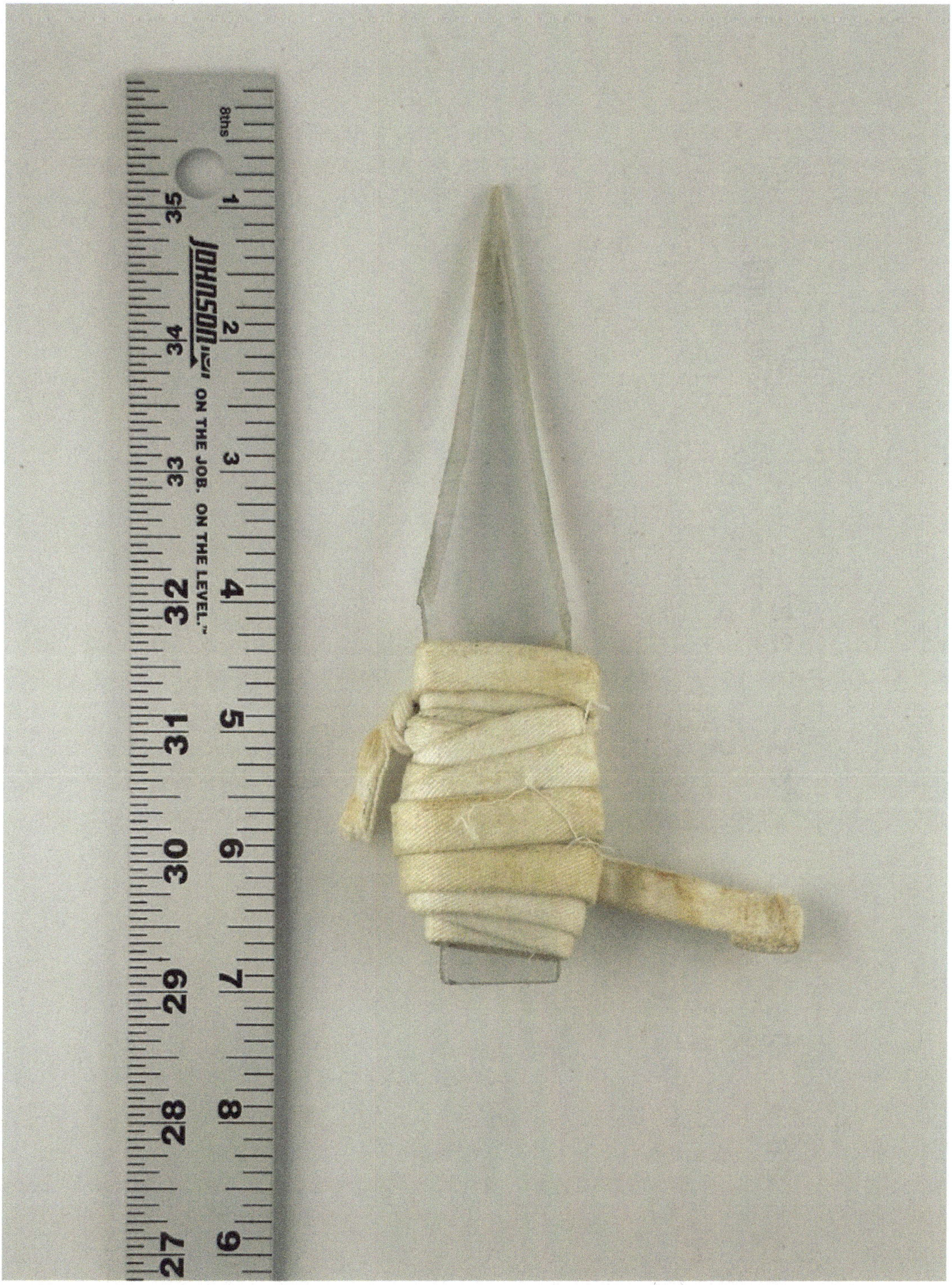
JOHNSON
ON THE JOB. ON THE LEVEL.™

JOHNSON
"ON THE JOB. ON THE LEVEL."

JOHNSON
ON THE JOB. ON THE LEVEL.
8ths

JOHNSON
"ON THE JOB. ON THE LEVEL."

JOHNSON
ON THE JOB. ON THE LEVEL.™

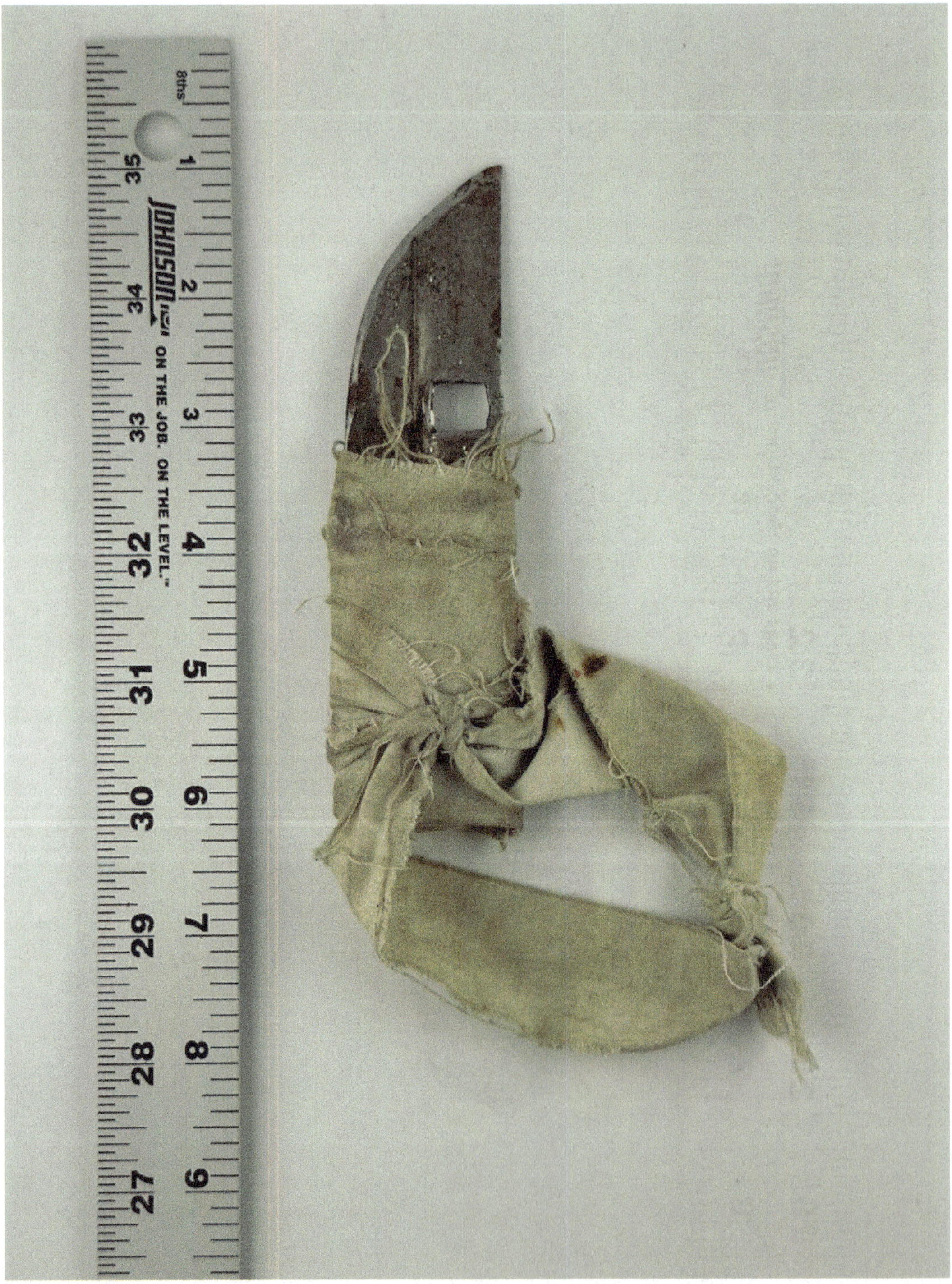
JOHNSON
ON THE JOB. ON THE LEVEL."

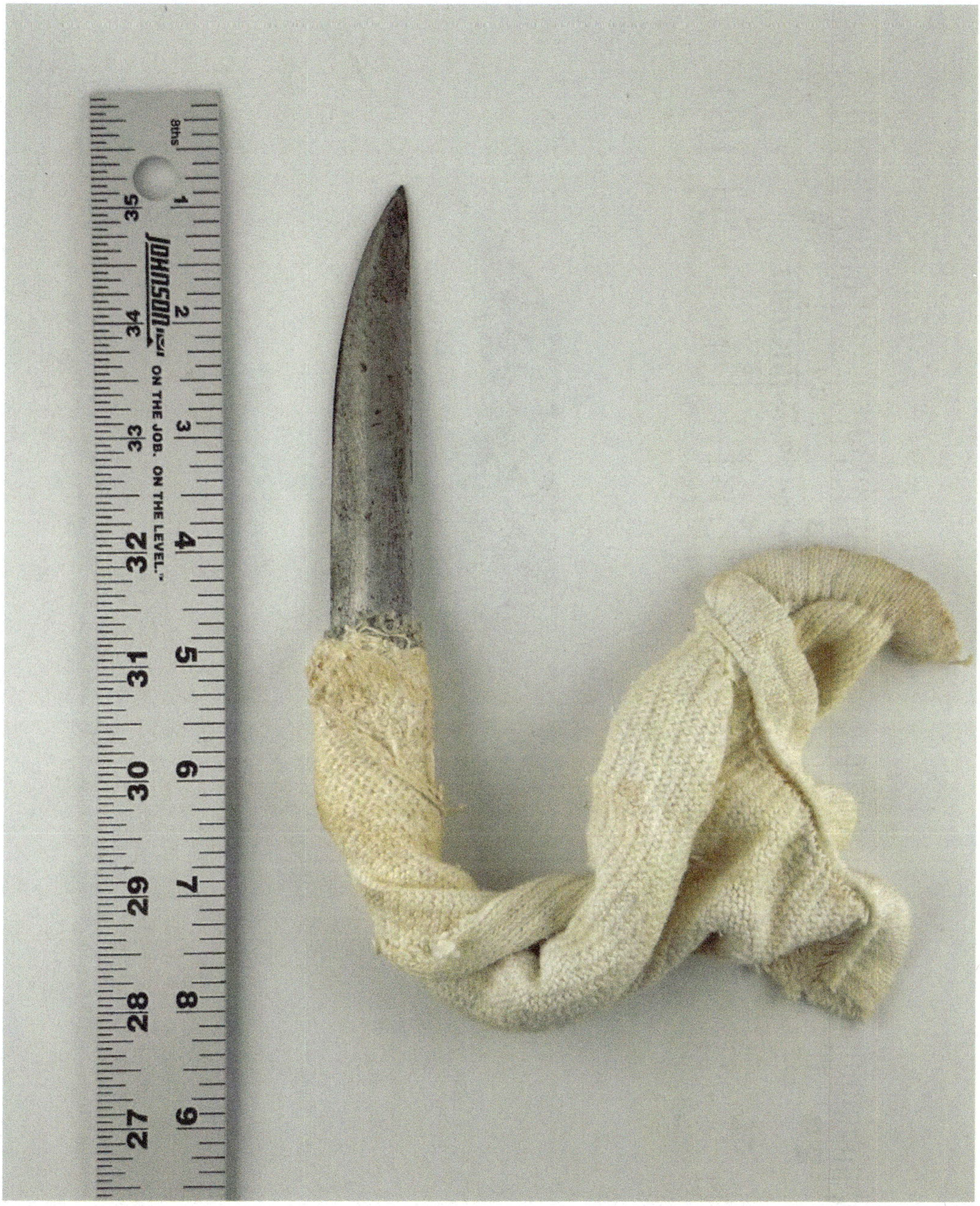
JOHNSON
ON THE JOB. ON THE LEVEL.

JOHNSON
ON THE JOB. ON THE LEVEL.™
8ths

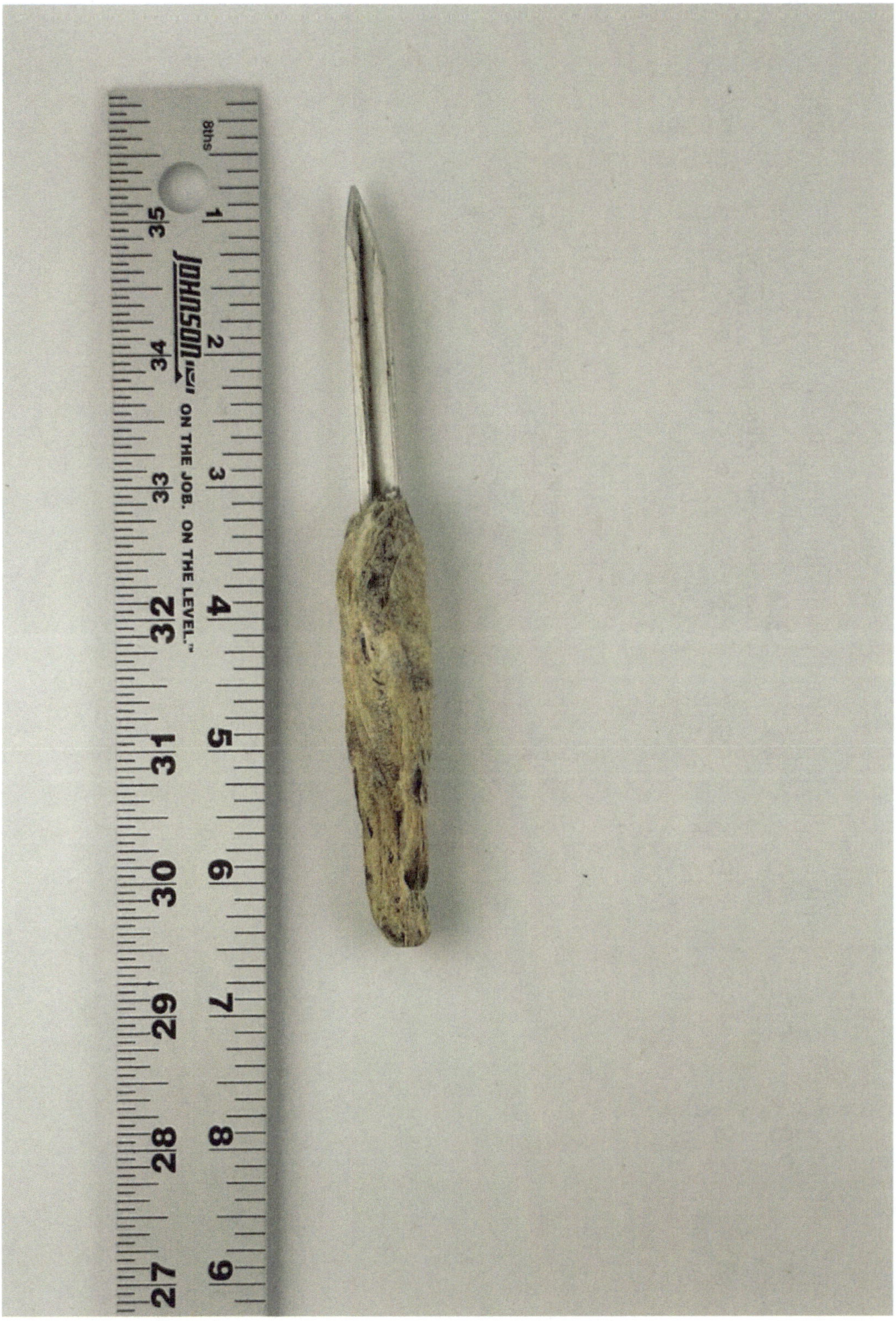
JOHNSON
"ON THE JOB. ON THE LEVEL."
8ths

JOHNSON
"ON THE JOB. ON THE LEVEL."

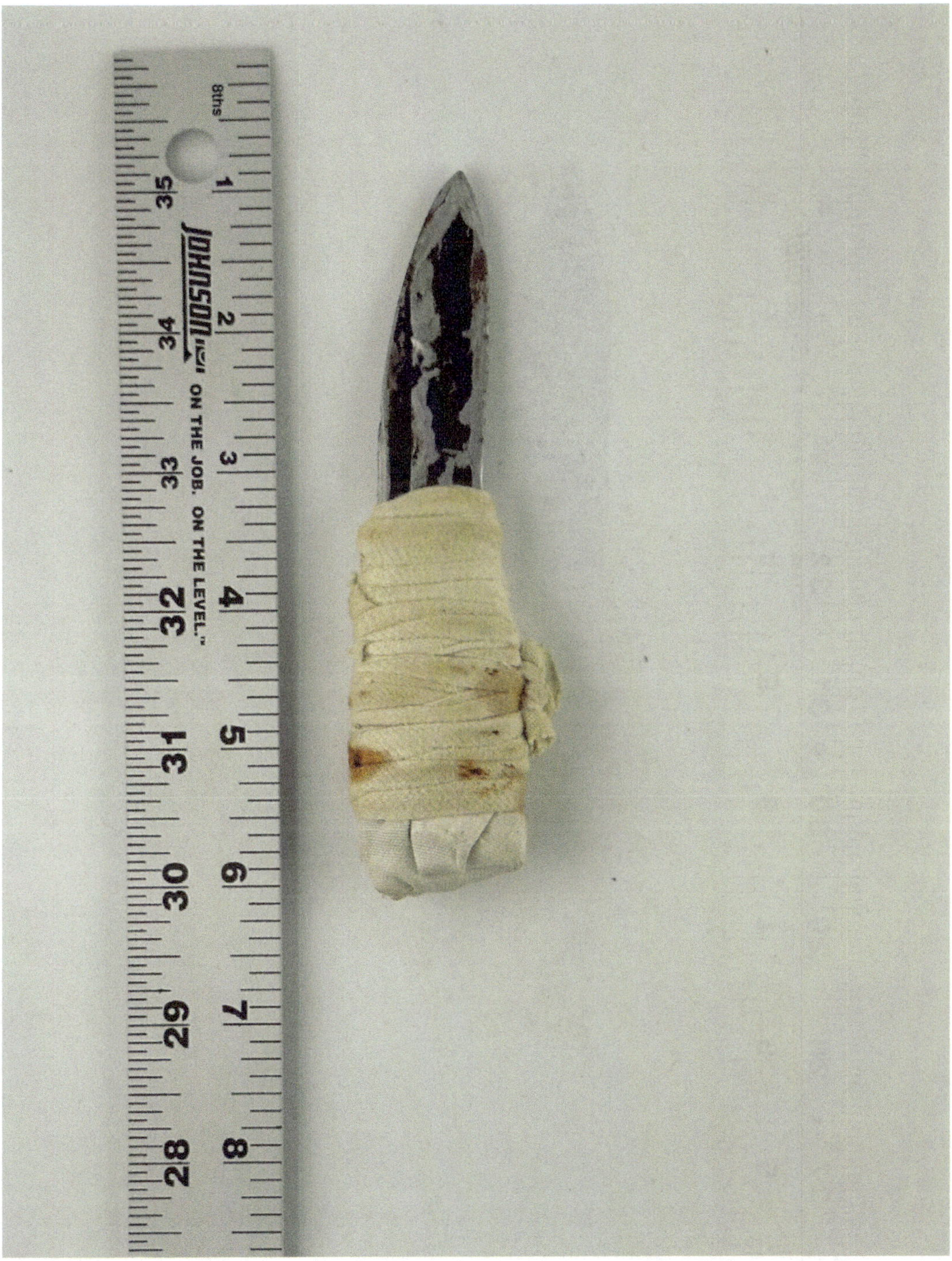
8ths
JOHNSON
"ON THE JOB. ON THE LEVEL."

JOHNSON
"ON THE JOB. ON THE LEVEL."

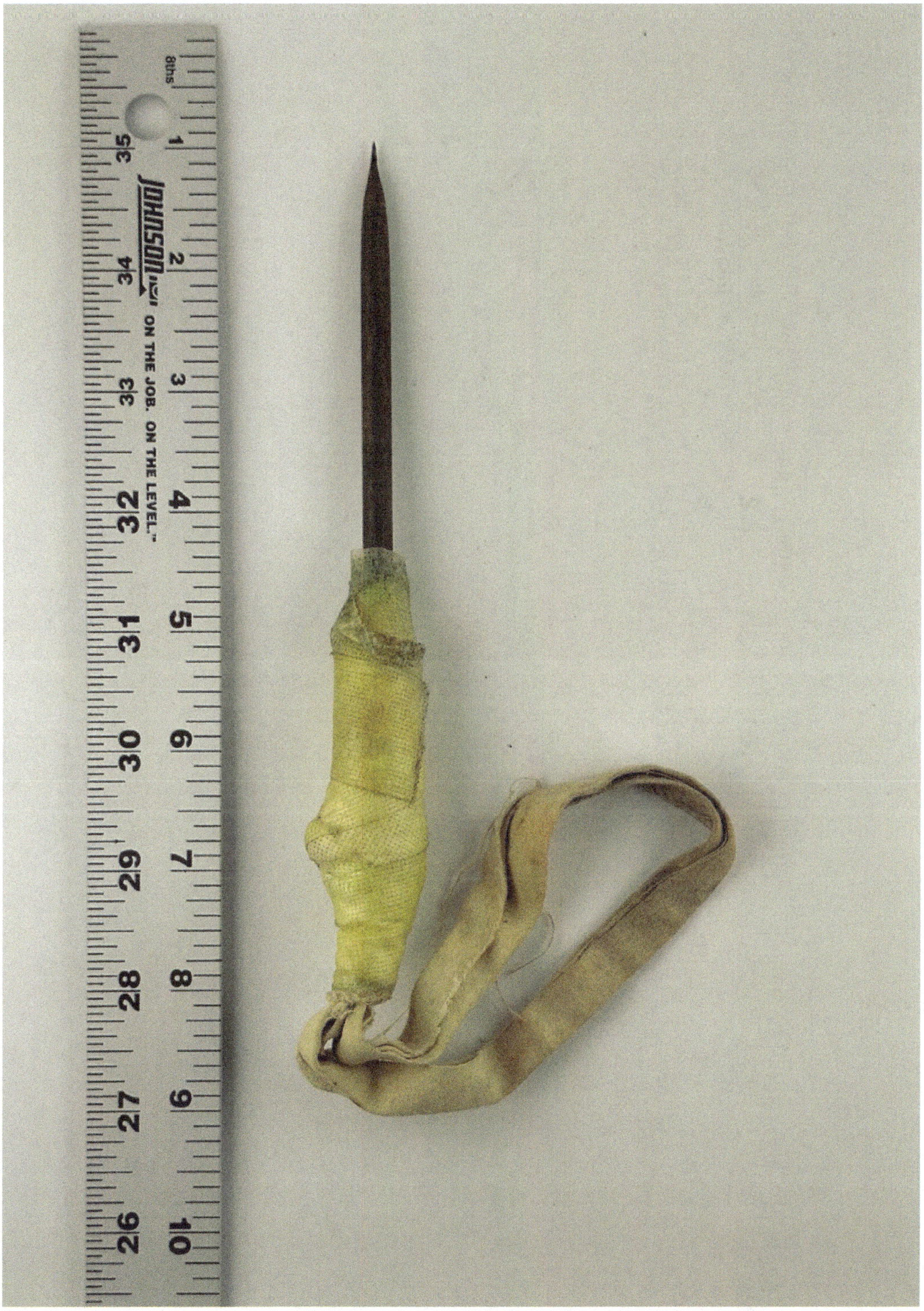
JOHNSON
ON THE JOB. ON THE LEVEL.™

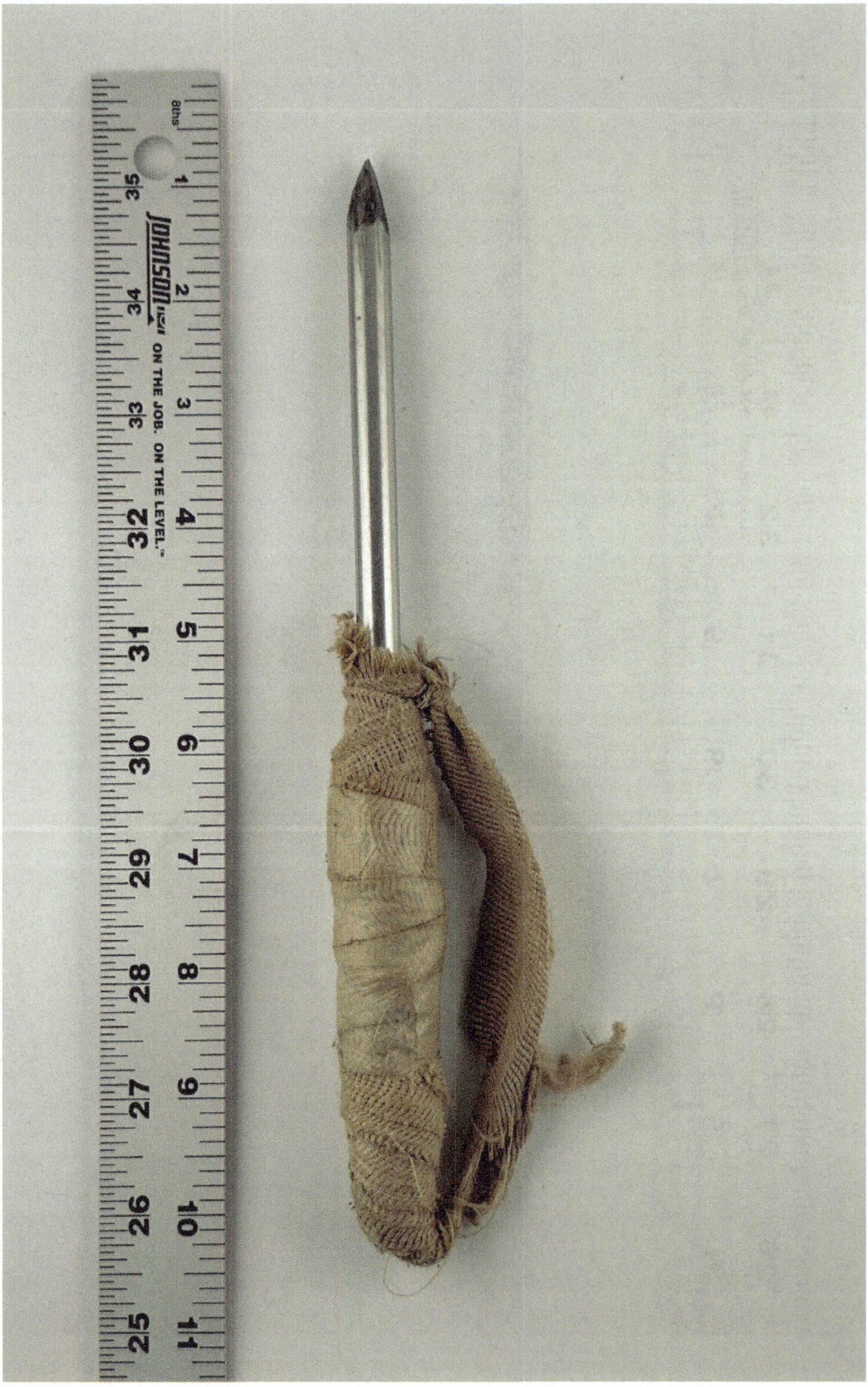
JOHNSON
"ON THE JOB. ON THE LEVEL."

JOHNSON
ON THE JOB. ON THE LEVEL.

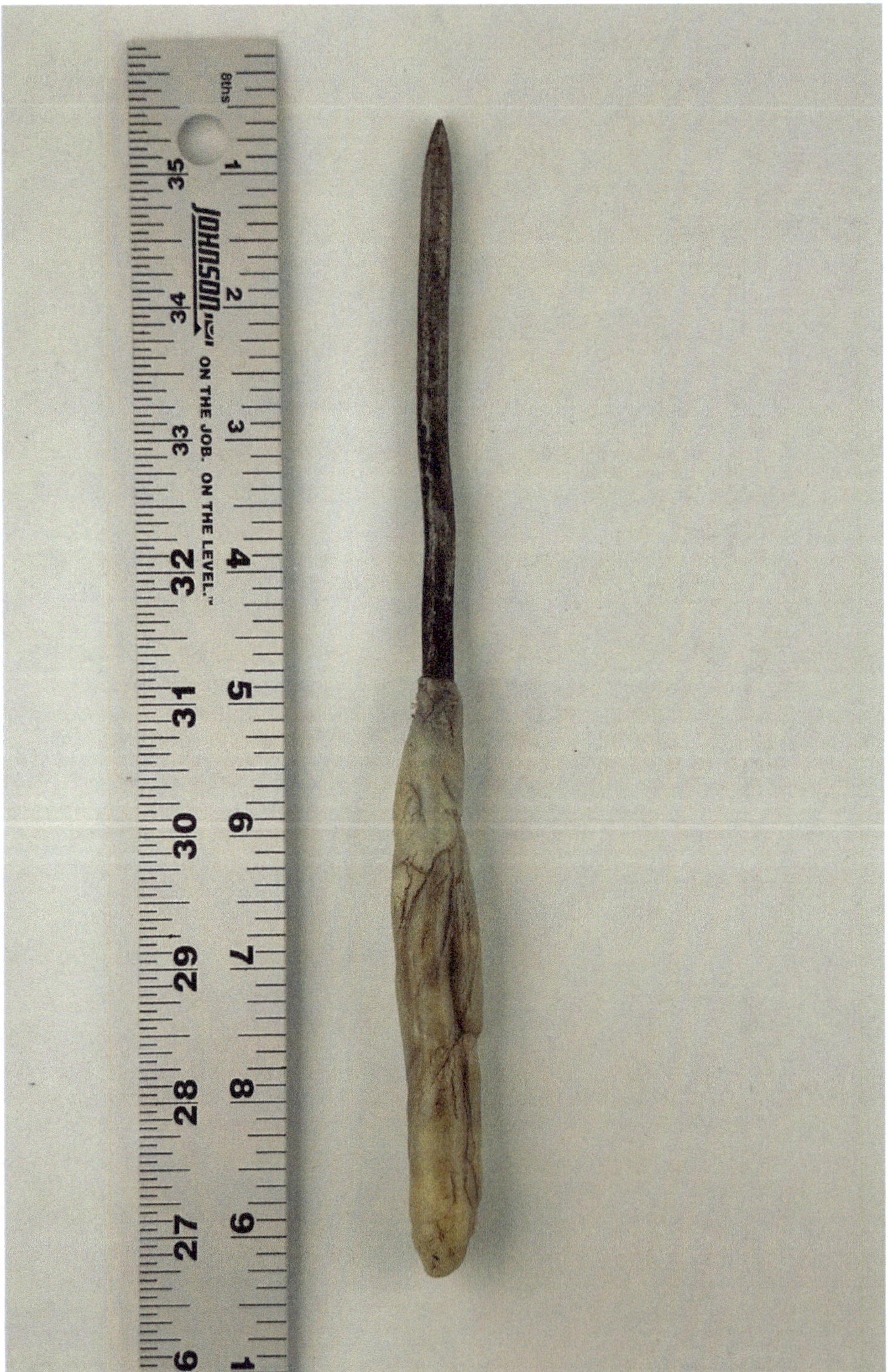
JOHNSON
ON THE JOB. ON THE LEVEL.™

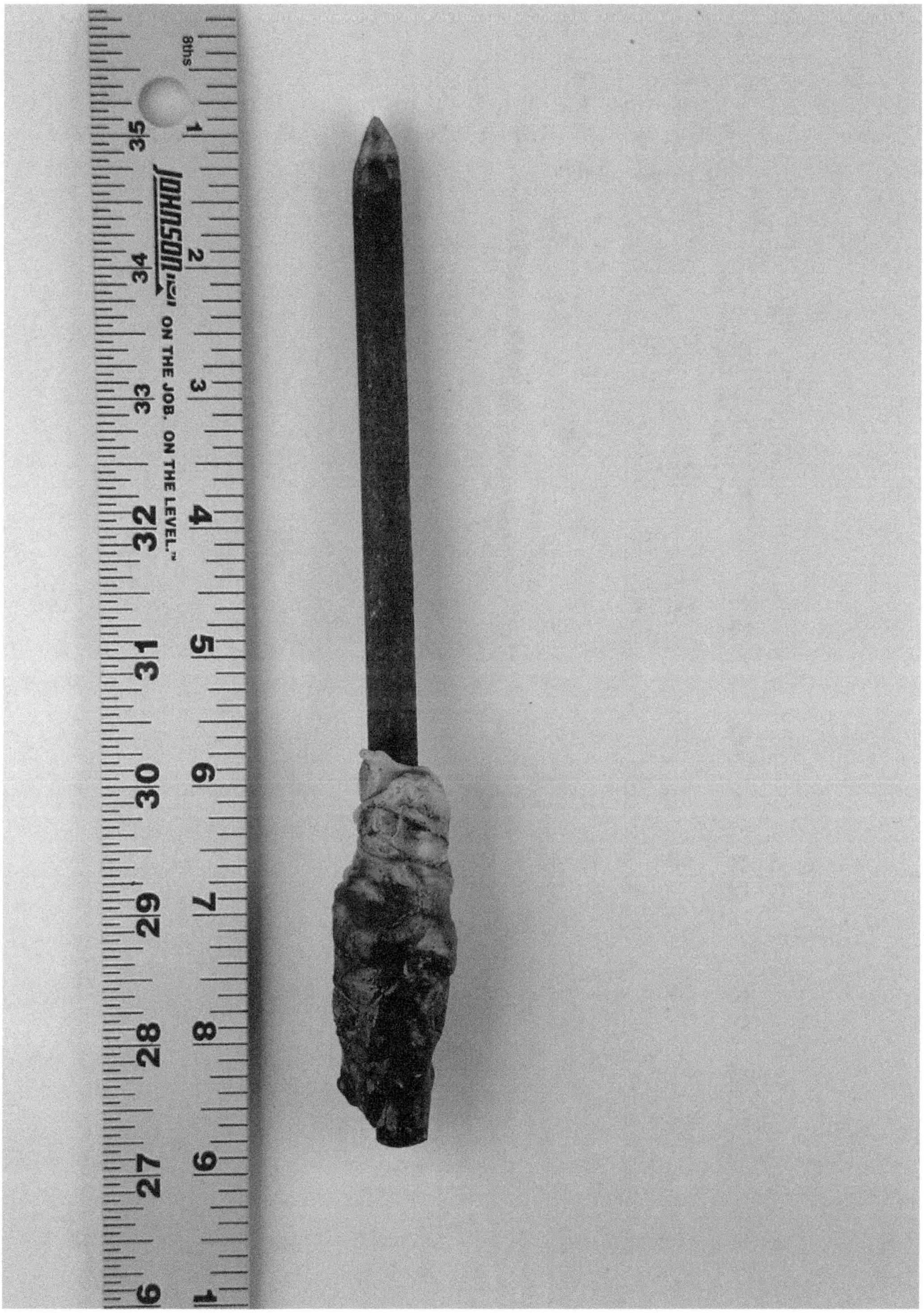
JOHNSON
ON THE JOB. ON THE LEVEL.™

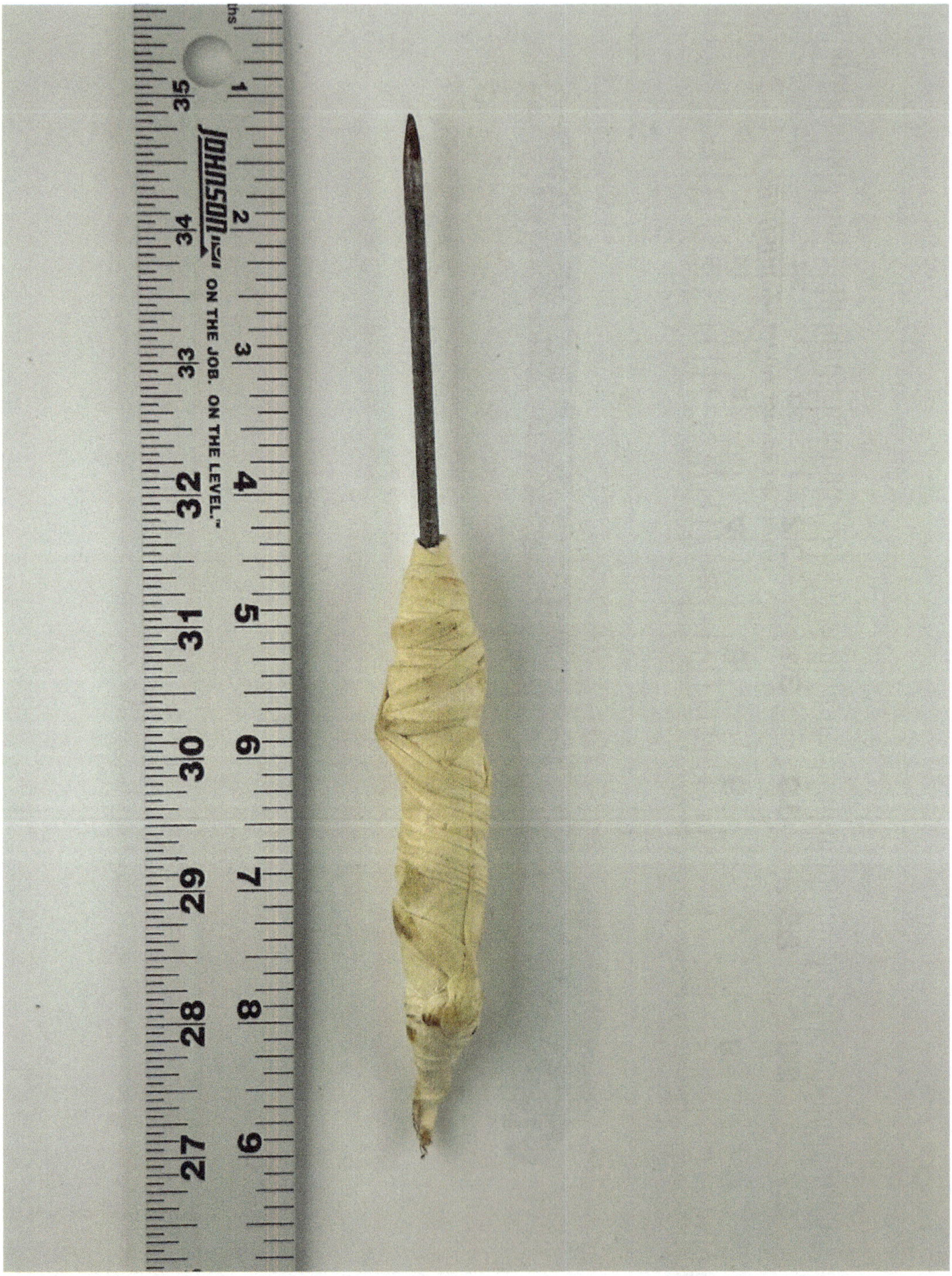
JOHNSON
"ON THE JOB. ON THE LEVEL."

JOHNSON
"ON THE JOB. ON THE LEVEL."
8ths

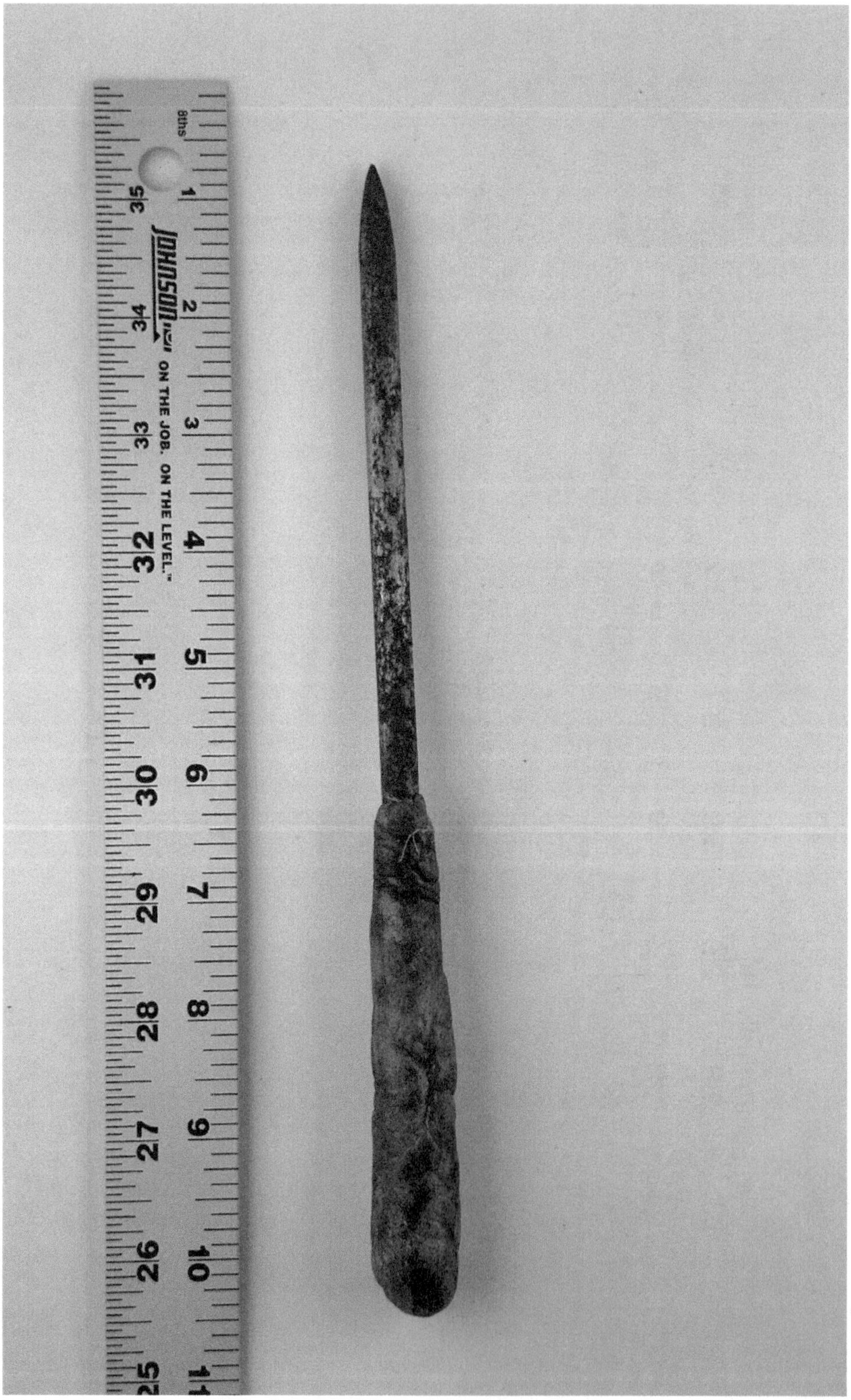
JOHNSON
ON THE JOB. ON THE LEVEL.

JOHNSON
"ON THE JOB. ON THE LEVEL."

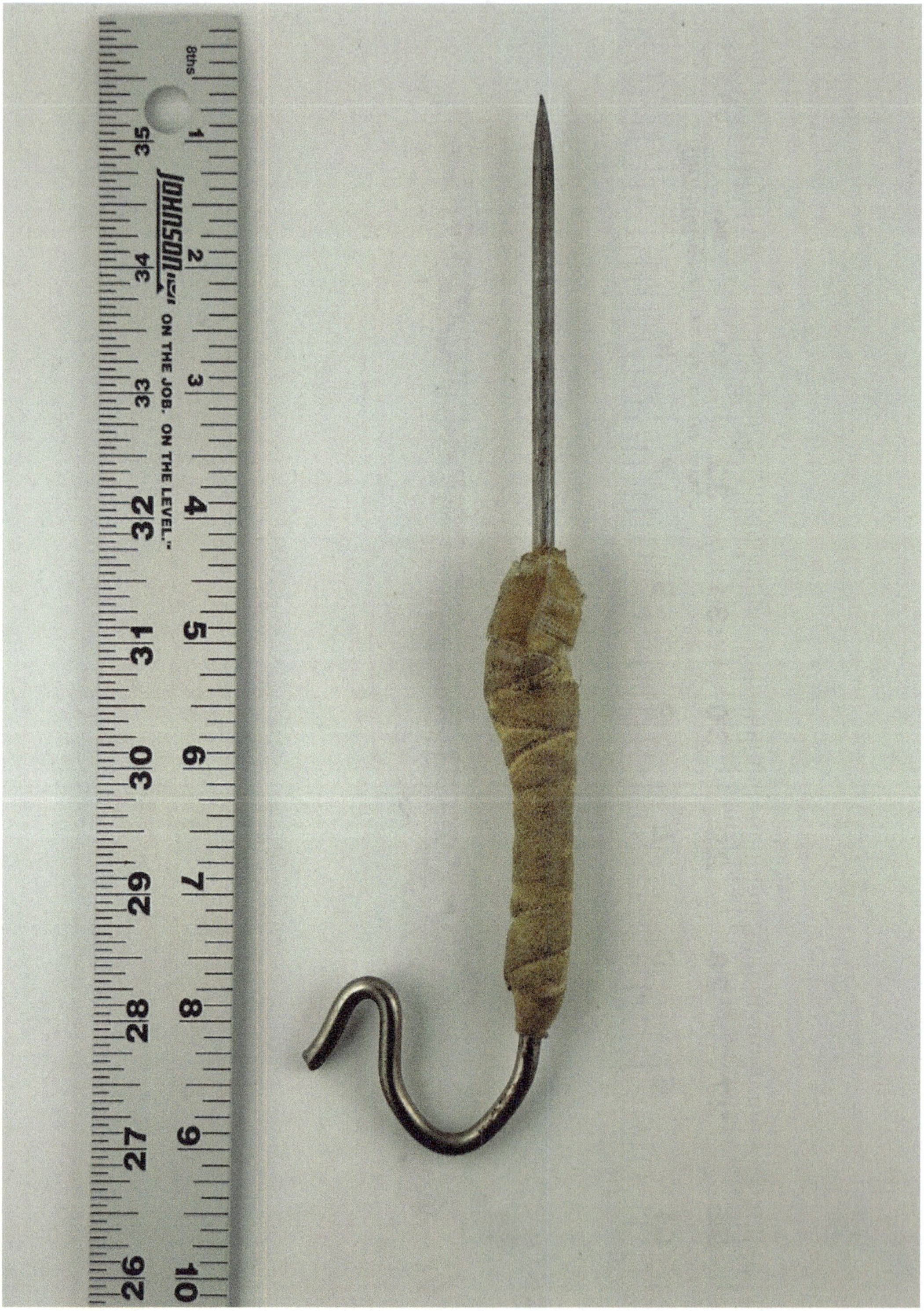
JOHNSON
ON THE JOB. ON THE LEVEL.

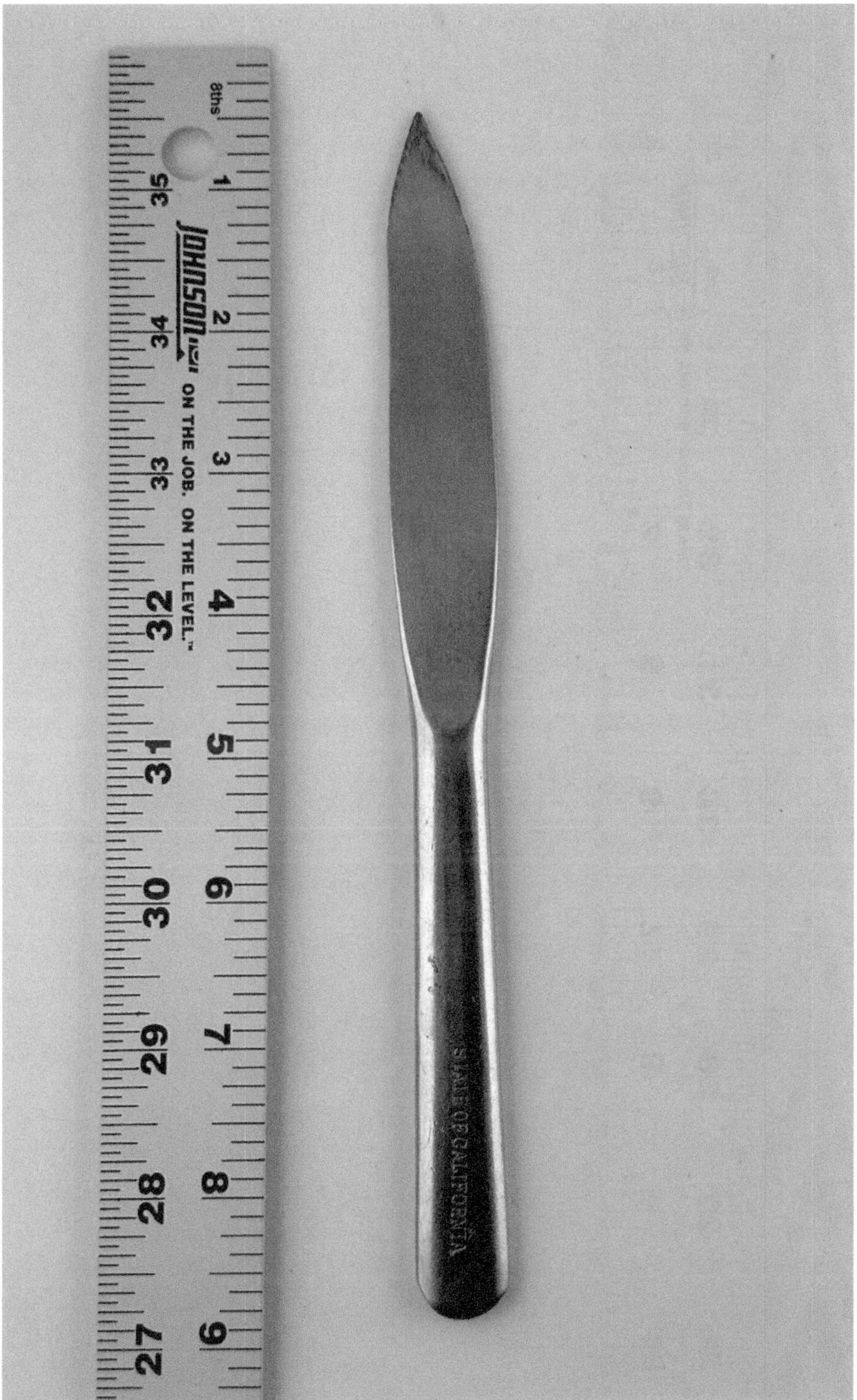
JOHNSON
ON THE JOB. ON THE LEVEL.™
STATE OF CALIFORNIA

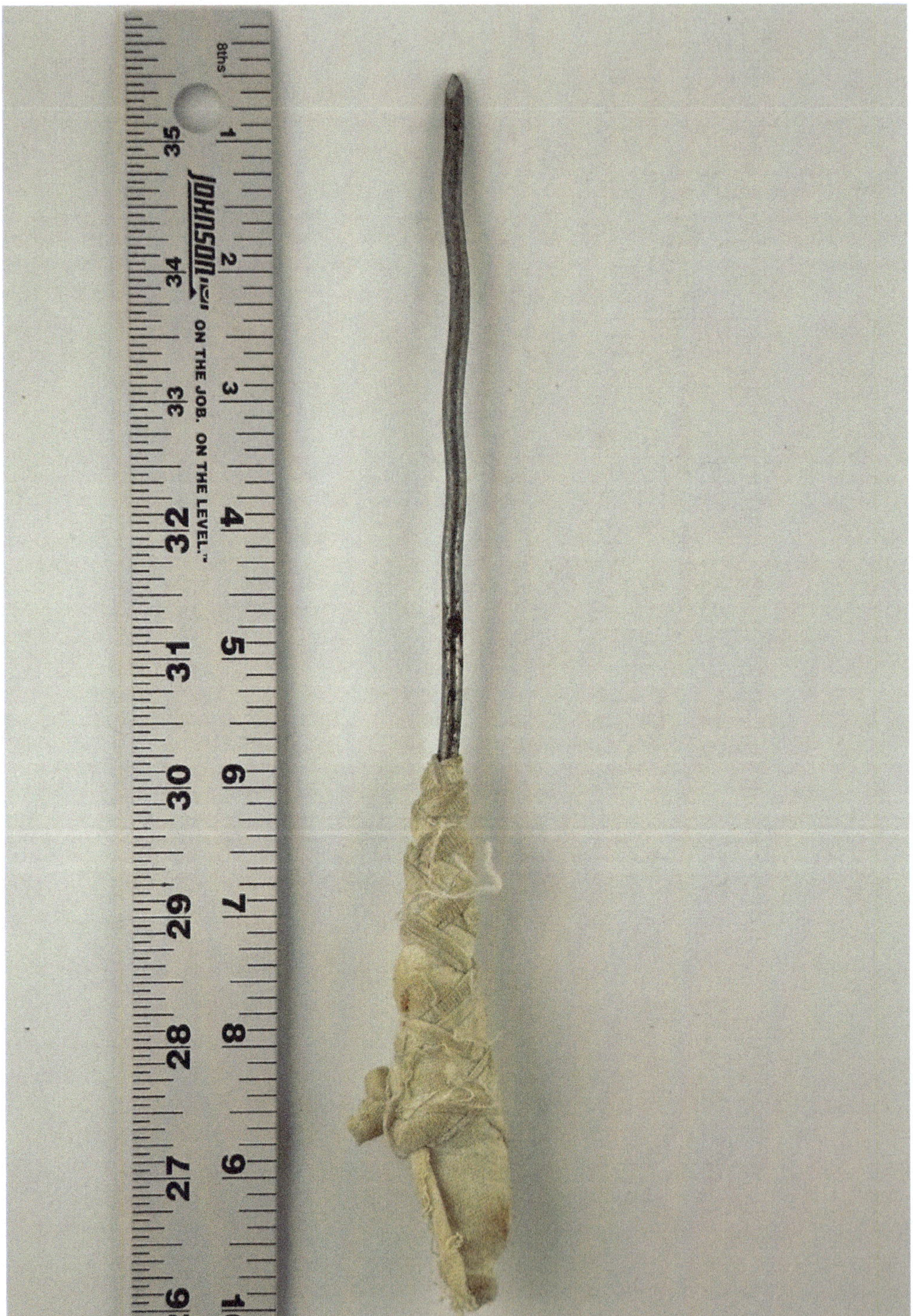
JOHNSON
"ON THE JOB. ON THE LEVEL."

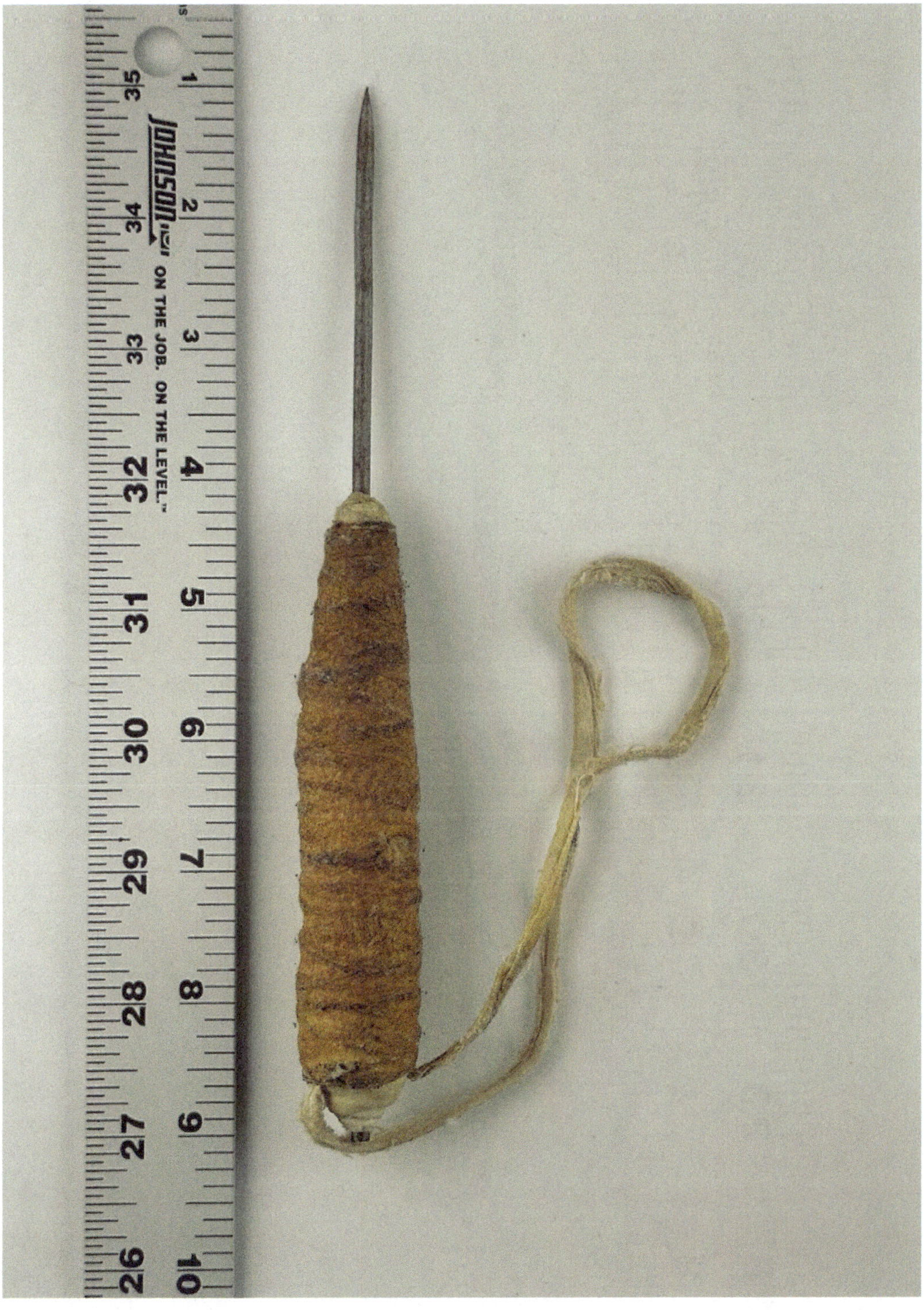
JOHNSON
ON THE JOB, ON THE LEVEL.™

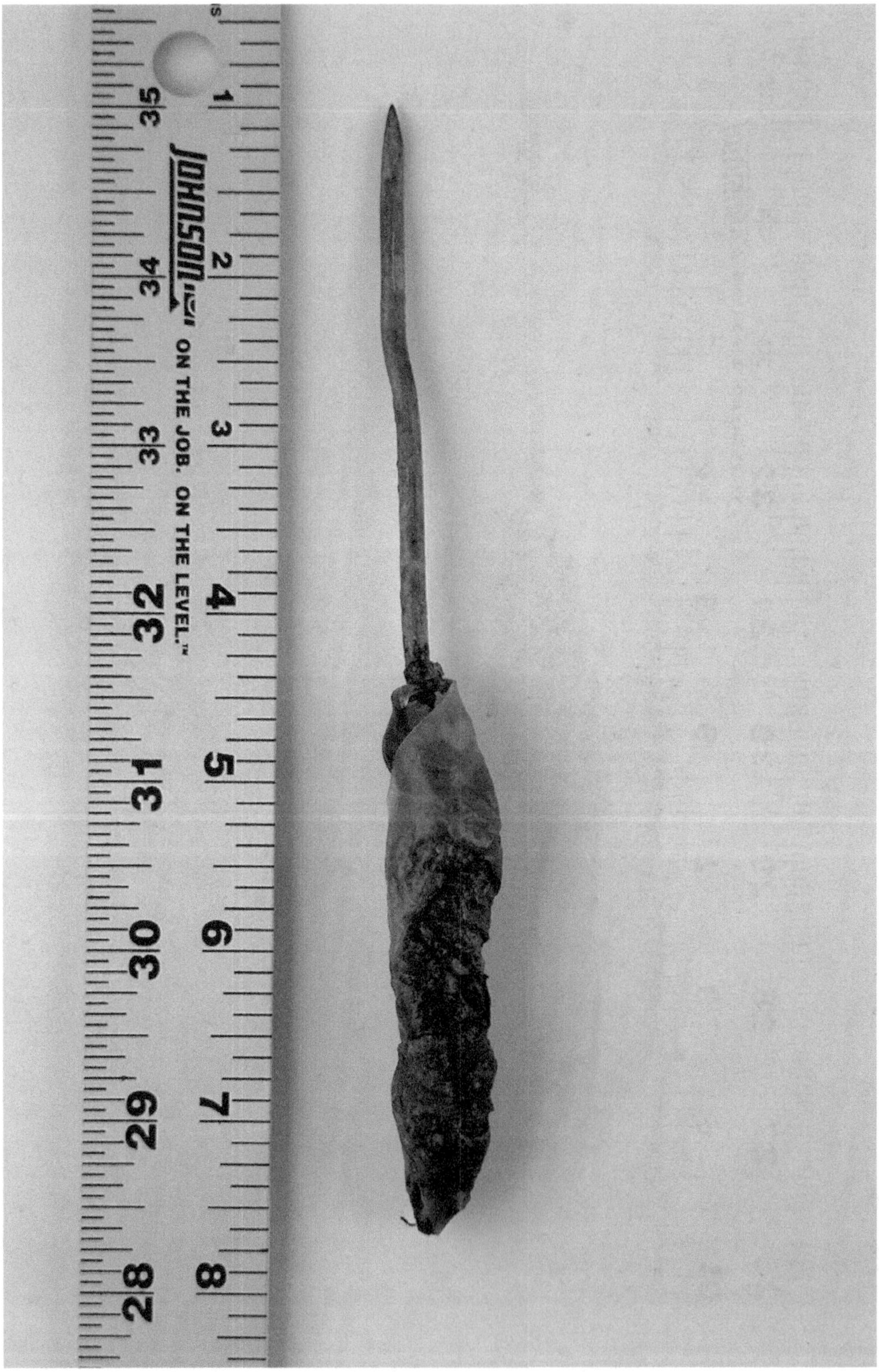
JOHNSON
ON THE JOB. ON THE LEVEL.™

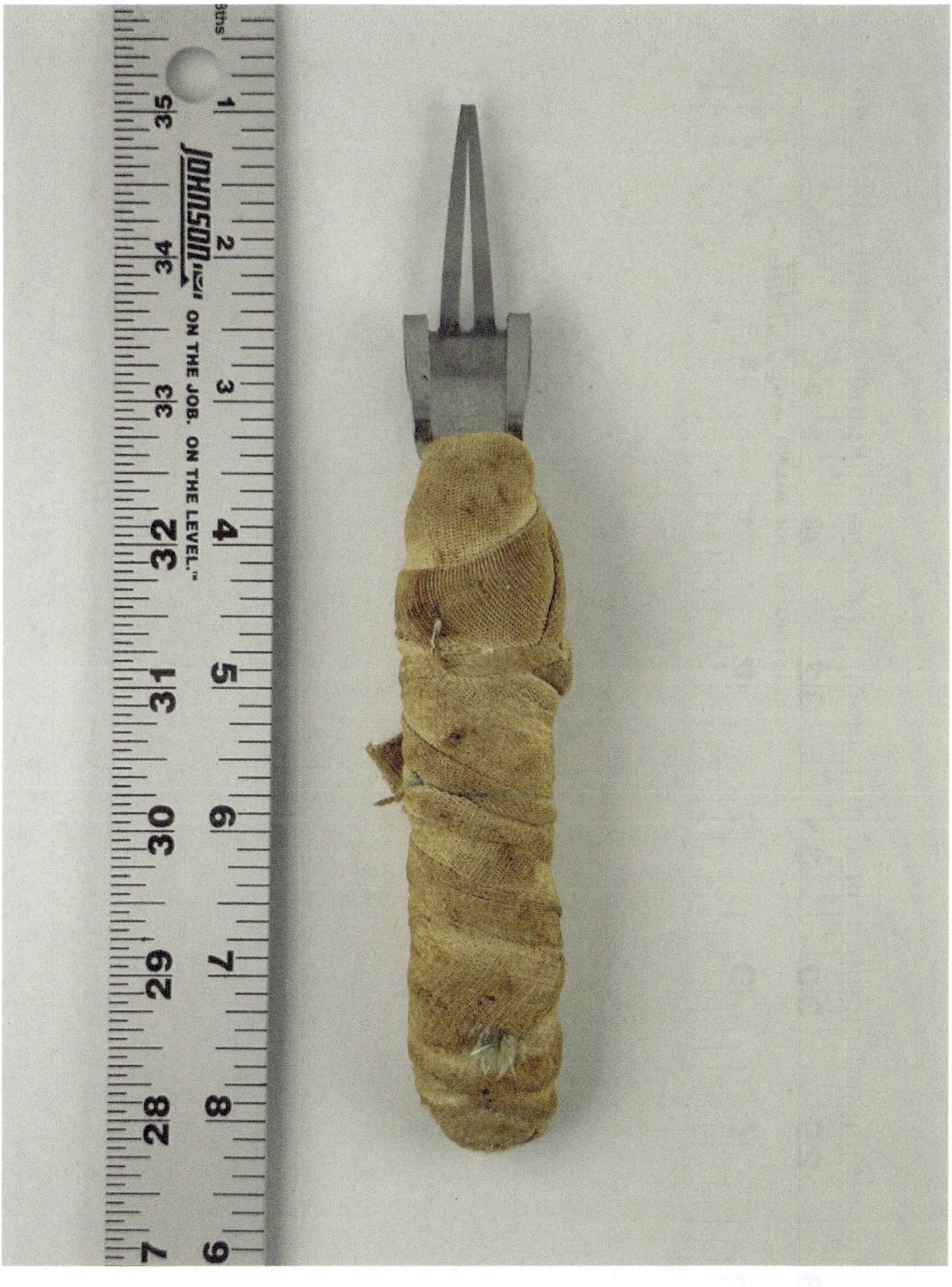
JOHNSON
"ON THE JOB. ON THE LEVEL."

8ths
JOHNSON
ON THE JOB. ON THE LEVEL.™

Notable California Prison Riots and Other Incidents

November 7, 2024: Six officers were injured, and three inmates were relocated after a disturbance at Kern Valley State Prison on Thursday. An inmate attacked an officer, leading staff to use chemical agents and physical force to subdue him. Two other inmates then assaulted staff, prompting further use of force. The situation was eventually controlled, and a weapon made by an inmate was recovered. The injured officers were treated at a hospital and have since been discharged.

February 1, 2024: On Thursday, authorities reported that eight corrections officers and one inmate were injured during a riot involving about 200 inmates at Ironwood State Prison in Blythe, Southern California. The disturbance began around 10 a.m. Wednesday during a contraband investigation when an inmate headbutted a staff member, leading other inmates to attack officers with fists and rocks. Officers responded with a warning shot and deployed chemical agents and non-lethal rounds. The injured were treated at an external hospital before returning to the prison, with the severity of their injuries undisclosed. Thirty inmates have been identified as directly involved, and the investigation is ongoing.

August 10, 2023: A riot broke out at Salinas Valley State Prison between the Blacks and Southerners. Four inmates received stab wounds and were transported to outside hospitals for treatment. The Southerners approached the Blacks and asked them to remove a Crip for stabbing a Mexican Mafia member a few weeks prior at another prison. The Blacks refused, so the Southerners stabbed the Crip with whom they had an issue, and the riot followed.

August 11, 2022: A riot at Tehachapi Prison left six inmates receiving treatment at outside hospitals. Officers used chemical agents and less lethal rounds to help quell the disturbance. Several inmate-manufactured weapons were recovered from the scene.

October 29, 2020: Twenty inmates were involved in a riot at Folsom Prison. Five inmates were transported to nearby hospitals to treat their injuries.

August 30, 2019: A riot involving 40 inmates erupted at Susanville Prison, resulting in nine inmates and four officers being transported to area hospitals for treatment.

August 29, 2019: A riot involving 50 inmates jumped off at California Men's Colony. Officers fired rounds from the Mini-14 rifle to stop the disturbance. Two inmates were taken to area hospitals for treatment.

August 28, 2019: A riot involving 40 inmates erupted at California Men's Colony. Four inmates got stabbed and slashed.

August 24, 2019: A riot involving 80 inmates kicked off at Richard J. Donovan Correctional Facility. Five inmates were injured and transported to area hospitals.

August 14, 2019: A riot involving 200 inmates at Soledad State Prison resulted in eight inmates getting treatment for injuries at area hospitals, and 50 others suffered minor injuries. Four inmate-manufactured weapons were recovered, and the tower officer fired rounds from the Mini-14 to help quell the violence.

July 18, 2019: To quell a riot involving 41 Salinas Valley State Prison inmates, guards discharged rounds from the Mini-14 rifle. Three inmates were stabbed and treated at outside hospitals.

July 18, 2019: A riot kicked off at Pleasant Valley State Prison involving 41 inmates. Guards fired rounds from the Mini-14 rifle to help quell the disturbance. Three inmates were stabbed and treated at area hospitals.

July 8, 2019: A riot involving 25 inmates jumped off at Salinas Valley State Prison. Four inmates were stabbed and transported to outside hospitals for treatment. Five inmate-manufactured weapons were recovered from the scene.

June 4, 2019: A riot involving 40 inmates broke out at Alder Creek Conservation Camp. Three inmates were taken to outside hospitals for treatment.

November 14, 2018: A riot involving 134 inmates jumped off at Pleasant Valley State Prison. Five inmates were transported to local hospitals.

November 14, 2018: A riot involving 80 inmates kicked off at Avenal State Prison. Six inmates were taken to area hospitals.

September 29, 2018: A riot at Avenal Prison left eleven inmates getting treatment at outside hospitals. Three of those inmates were life flighted to the hospital during that Saturday morning.

March 25, 2018: A riot involving 65 inmates broke out at California Correctional Institution. Guards fired several rounds from the Mini-14 rifle to stop the rampage. One inmate was shot in his buttocks. Five inmates were transported to area hospitals or treatment.

September 24, 2017: Guards used rubber bullets to help stop a riot involving 160 inmates at California Men's Colony. Nine inmates were stabbed and were transported to an area hospital. One inmate later died from his wounds.

August 17, 2017: A riot involving 350 inmates kicked off at Sierra Conservation Center. Guards fired several Mini-14 rounds to stop the melee. Seven inmates were transported to area hospitals for treatment.

July 12, 2017: A riot involving 20 inmates erupted at Salinas Valley State Prison, resulting in five inmates getting treatment at area hospitals.

May 24, 2017: 97 inmates rioted at Pelican Bay State Prison, resulting in five inmates getting shot. Eight officers and seven inmates were taken to area hospitals for treatment after the battle.

March 15, 2017: A riot at Susanville Prison left six officers and one inmate injured. An inmate attacked an officer in the dining hall, and then 30 inmates joined the attack and smashed food trays on the heads of some officers.

March 7, 2017: A riot involving 110 inmates erupted at California State Prison, Corcoran.

February 8, 2017: A riot involving 125 inmates erupted at Kern Valley State Prison. Five inmates were injured and taken to area hospitals for treatment.

February 7, 2017: A riot involving 125 inmates broke out at Kern Valley State Prison. Seven inmate-manufactured weapons were recovered.

December 22, 2016: A riot at Susanville Prison erupted that involved 100 inmates. Four inmates were hospitalized due to the violence, with one suffering from a gunshot wound to his buttocks.

May 27, 2016: A riot at High Desert State Prison involving 65 inmates resulted in five inmates being transported to outside hospitals for treatment. The riot started on the recreation yard of Facility D, which houses Level IV inmates. 21 inmate-manufactured weapons were recovered from the scene.

August 27, 2015: A riot involving 90 inmates happened at Salinas Valley State Prison in the morning. Two inmates were sliced with tomahawks and had to be treated at area hospitals.

August 16, 2015: A riot at Susanville Prison involving 45 inmates in the dining hall resulted in one inmate getting killed by an officer with a Mini-14 rifle after four warning shots.

August 12, 2015: Following the murder of inmate Hugo Pinell by White inmates, a riot erupted between them and the Black inmates. Seventy inmates were engaged in the disturbance, necessitating several warning shots from the Mini-14 rifle to suppress the turmoil.

March 20, 2015: 60 inmates rioted for five minutes at Calipatria State Prison during the evening yard. Two inmates were taken to area hospitals for treatment.

January 8, 2015: A riot at Calipatria State Prison left 30 inmates and 20 officers wounded; 1 inmate was killed after being shot in the abdomen. The mayhem lasted for about 45 minutes before being quelled. Twenty minutes after getting the riot under control, another group of inmates attacked the officers again.

June 3, 2013: 40 inmates were involved in a riot on the exercise yard at Wasco State Prison that left one dead. Three inmates were taken to a nearby hospital.

December 8, 2012: 115 inmates were involved in a riot at Calipatria State Prison, leaving nine inmates getting treatment at area hospitals.

October 6, 2012: A riot involving more than 460 Blacks and Southerners occurred at Ironwood State Prison, resulting in seven inmates going to area hospitals.

September 19, 2012: 65 inmates were involved in a riot on the New Folsom Prison exercise yard, leaving 13 hospitalized. Eight inmates were stabbed, and one was shot by an officer.

February 10, 2012: 175 inmates were involved in a riot on the exercise yard at San Quentin. Dozens of inmates were stabbed and sliced during the violent melee.

December 7, 2011: 50 inmates were rioting at New Folsom Prison on the Level 4 yard. Seven rounds from the Mini-14 were fired to try and stop the violence. Nine inmates were taken to area hospitals for treatment; several were stabbed.

June 7, 2011: A riot involving 50 inmates at Avenal Prison resulted in five receiving medical care at outside hospitals.

May 23, 2011: A riot at San Quentin involving 200 inmates erupted in the chow hall, and four were stabbed.

May 20, 2011: 150 inmates were involved in a riot at Folsom Prison. Two inmates were stabbed, and numerous others were taken to area hospitals for treatment.

October 19, 2010: 120 inmates were involved in a riot at Calipatria State Prison, and 14 were injured. The Mini-14 rifle was used to help suppress the violence.

August 27, 2010: 200 inmates were involved in a riot at Folsom Prison. The fighting started at the handball court and escalated quickly. Seven inmates were taken to area hospitals for treatment.

June 12, 2010: 39 inmates were involved in a riot at Calipatria State Prison, and 37 were injured. One inmate died as a result of the fighting.

September 21, 2009: 193 inmates rioted at Avenal Prison, resulting in 24 inmates receiving treatment at outside hospitals. 30 inmate-manufactured weapons were recovered from the bloody scene.

August 15, 2009: A riot at Avenal Prison, involving 70 Blacks and Southerners, resulted in several inmates getting stabbed.

August 8, 2009: A large riot at Chino State Prison between the Black inmates and the Southerners left more than 240 injured and two buildings destroyed. 55 inmates were hospitalized. The violence left the prison in a state of emergency.

June 21, 2009: A riot broke out at Corcoran State Prison involving 75 inmates. 11 inmates were stabbed and treated at area hospitals. 28 inmate-manufactured weapons were recovered. This melee is commonly referred to as the Father's Day Massacre, and it was a battle between the Southerners and Northerners.

December 30, 2007: 200 Blacks and Southerners were involved in a riot at Chino State Prison that lasted for 90 minutes. 27 inmates were taken to local hospitals. Inmates wrapped six shards of glass with cloth on one end and used them as bangers.

January 13, 2006: A riot at San Quentin in the chow hall injured 23 inmates and two correctional officers.

September 22, 2005: A riot at Chino State Prison involving 200 Blacks and Southerners resulted in 8 injuries.

August 18, 2005: A vicious riot erupted at Calipatria State Prison, leaving one inmate dead, 16 officers wounded, and 25 inmates wounded. At around 1500 hours, an inmate was being searched by an officer, and when an inmate-manufactured weapon was discovered on him, the inmate used it to stab the officer in the head. After the officer was stabbed, dozens of his fellow gang members attacked the rest of the officers. The mayhem lasted for about four hours until it was quelled. Two inmates were shot during this uprising, one in the stomach and one in the head.

August 9, 2005: A riot at San Quentin involved 80 White and Mexican inmates, in which 42 were injured. One inmate received a large gash on his face from a tomahawk, and several lock-in-a-sock weapons were found.

February 24, 2005: A riot at Tehachapi Prison involving 400 Blacks and Southerners lasted about 40 minutes. Several inmate-manufactured weapons were recovered.

April 8, 2002: A riot at Folsom Prison between 80 Northerners and Southerners resulted in 25 of them getting injured. For 12 weeks prior, these warring factions had been separated, but on April 8, they were released on the main yard together.

December 21, 2001: 400 inmates rioted at Lancaster Prison for 15 minutes. 26 homemade weapons were recovered, and six inmates were stabbed. Several warning shots were fired to help quell the violence. Two inmates suffered collapsed lungs after being stabbed.

July 29, 2000: 120 Southerners and Peckerwoods rioted at Lancaster Prison, resulting in ten injuries.

February 23, 2000: 200 Blacks and Southerners were involved in one of the bloodiest riots in California history. The riot occurred on Bravo Yard and lasted 30 minutes at Pelican Bay Prison. There were 24 rounds fired from the Mini-14 to help stop the outbreak of violence. Nineteen inmates were stabbed, 15 were shot, and one was killed. 89 inmate-manufactured weapons were recovered. 16 ambulances arrived at the prison to help transport the injured.

June 5, 1995: Five Crips rushed into the program office while the door was unlocked at 0930 hours and attacked the officers inside with inmate-manufactured weapons. Eight officers were taken to outside hospitals for treatment, with several getting stabbed. A female sergeant suffered severe stab wounds during the violent attack. The motive for this attack is unknown, but officers shot and killed an inmate two months prior during a fight. This attack changed the California Department of Corrections and Rehabilitation's policy on Level IV yards because, after this, they installed fences separating the program office from the rest of the prison yard. They also sectioned the yard off with two buildings in one section and three in the other.

November 1986: An unclassified FBI document states that an inmate was discovered with dynamite at Tehachapi Prison. The FBI believes the dynamite was for use against other inmates.

December 1985: An unclassified FBI document states that large quantities of C-4 explosives were smuggled into Folsom Prison. Correctional officers discovered these explosives but believed more was still circulating in the prison.

June 20, 1982: One of the largest riots in San Quentin's history resulted in injuries to 22 inmates and four correctional officers. Seven inmates got stabbed, and 15 had injuries from shotgun blasts from officers. Three prison gangs were involved in this riot.

December 6, 1979: Two inmates were killed and 17 injured in a riot involving 80 inmates at Soledad State Prison. A group of Black inmates attacked the Whites and Southerners.

August 21, 1971: This marks the deadliest day in San Quentin's history, with three officers and three inmates losing their lives on this fateful afternoon.

January 13, 1970: On this day at the max row yard at Soledad State Prison, three Black inmates were shot and killed. One of these inmates was W. L. Nolen, a prison boxing legend and a plaintiff against the California Department of Corrections in a civil case. This watershed incident sparked violence, leading to 19 more killings of officers and inmates.

September 24, 1937: During a riot at Folsom Prison, inmates stabbed Warden Clarence Larkin 12 times, leading to his fatal injury. In the course of this incident, inmates held Warden Larkin hostage. Officer Martin endeavored to rescue him but was killed by inmates. The aftermath of this riot saw the loss of four lives: two staff members and two inmates.

November 24, 1927: A riot among 1,200 inmates at Folsom Prison resulted in the National Guard being called in along with two tanks. The inmates took five officers hostage. Company "E" of the 184th Infantry Division entered the prison with bayonets on their rifles in a skirmish line. The rioters quickly surrendered after this show of force by the 184th Infantry Division.

March 3, 1925: Two inmates died over ten days of riots at San Quentin Prison. Guards were ordered to shoot to kill over any new signs of trouble by Warden Smith.

About the Author

Eric has emerged as a highly accomplished investor and Day Trader, engaging in trading activities with a substantial value of stocks annually. He enjoys the status of a dedicated husband and father, being blessed with four wonderful daughters who hold a special place in his heart. Eric's existence revolves around upholding the virtues of a devout Christian, a devoted husband, and a caring father guided by the grace of God. His journey has been transformative, considering his challenging upbringing, and he now stands as an illustrious testament to the boundless possibilities achievable through faith in God.

Eric joined a criminal street gang as a teenager, and he was eventually arrested and put in a cage at the Long Beach City Jail. He dropped out of Jordan High School in Long Beach, California, in the 10th grade. Eric eventually got on the right path by the Grace of God and obtained his GED the same month that he would have graduated. He joined the United States Coast Guard at 18, and after four years of faithful service, he was honorably discharged.

The following is an excerpt from his autobiography: "California Prison Confessions." "It was a typical beautiful summer night in Long Beach, California, and the three young teens fighting in the musty garage starkly contrasted the night's serenity. A teen called

Bones was thrown against a wall, and a muscular teenager nicknamed E Double (me) rushed towards him and violently punched him in his lower back. Another youth named Tim Loc held Bones against the wall during this attack. E Double's knuckles landed with a thick-sounding thud as Bones grimaced and moaned in pain from each successive blow.

There's a look of pain and fear in Bone's eyes as E Double mercilessly lands blow after blow to his kidneys. E Double has spent years hitting the heavy bag in his garage, so his punches are devastating for his age. The beating lasted a minute, and the two teens stopped attacking the unfortunate victim. Amazingly, they all shook hands and embraced each other. We were all friends, and this was our modest gang initiation into our small clique called Six Feet Under."

Our tiny neighborhood gang in North Long Beach, California, had several members of various races: White, Black, and Hispanic. The definition of a criminal street gang according to the California Penal Code is as follows:

"As used in this chapter, 'criminal street gang' means any ongoing organization, association, or group of three or more persons, whether formal or informal, having as one of its primary activities the commission of one or more of the criminal acts… having a common name or common identifying sign or symbol, and whose members individually or collectively engage in or have engaged in a pattern of criminal gang activity," California Penal Code 186.22(f).

Some of our associates committed serious crimes such as burglaries, drug sales, stealing cars, carrying guns, vandalism, and assaulting people. Although we were nothing but young punks, we were a criminal street gang according to the California Penal Code. The FBI did a study entitled "Street-Gang Mentality: A Mosaic of Remorseless Violence and Relentless Loyalty." I want to quote a relevant part concerning young males who do not have a father or other positive male role models in their lives while growing up:

"All gang members lacked male role models in their households, and when they lived with their mothers, they were rarely home because of work schedules. Gang members often lived temporarily with various people. All but one gang member reported that one or more immediate family members had a criminal history or abused drugs. Gangs attracted them because of their loyalty, stability, and sense of group identity."

There is an epidemic in this country of boys masquerading as men who don't take their responsibilities as fathers seriously. Many fathers aren't involved in their children's lives; if they are, they are a horrible example of what a real man should be. One of the main factors in young men ending up in the penal system is the lack of a father or, at the very least, a positive male role model when they were growing up. Absentee fathers are causing society to pay a high price for their selfish and callous actions.

Every day, I strive to be the best dad to the four beautiful daughters God has blessed me with. I live by the motto, "Be the man you needed as a child." I will not allow the actions of emotionally abusive people to define who I am or hinder my advancement in life. You can choose to be bitter or better. I strive for excellence because living well is the best response to abusive people.

Eric Sturgess
God bless you and yours.
Romans 10:9-13

For those seeking to connect with Eric or gather additional insights about the California Prison Book Series, please visit his official website: www.PrisonPanos.com.

Explore The Book Collection

Eric "Superman" Sturgess offers several books that showcase his extensive collection of prison art and related subjects:

Prison Paños: Ink on Cloth: This book features the top 50 paños from the world's largest private collection, highlighting intricate artworks drawn on linen, handkerchiefs, and bandannas.

California Prison Slang Dictionary: A comprehensive guide to the unique slang used within California's prison system.

California Prison Inmate Weapons: An exploration of the various weapons crafted by inmates, providing insight into prison ingenuity and survival tactics.

California Prison Slang Dictionary, Second Edition: An updated version of the original dictionary, offering expanded content on prison vernacular.

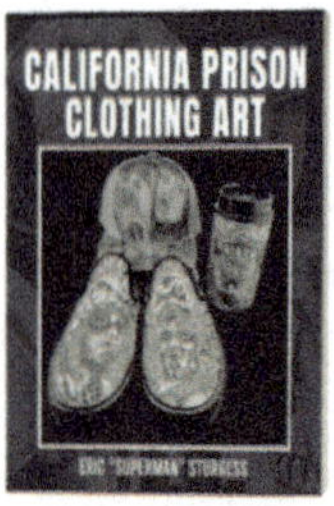

California Prison Clothing Art: A captivating collection showcasing artistic designs created by inmates on clothing items, reflecting life behind bars.

Texas Jail Art: Ink on Cloth: A powerful display of intricate ink art created on fabric by Texas inmates, blending cultural expression with personal stories.

California Prison Envelope Art: A unique compilation of artistic envelope designs by prisoners, depicting emotions and creative resilience.

California Prison Inmate Art: A vibrant portrayal of inmate artistry, offering a glimpse into their perspectives and cultural influences.

Prison Paños II: Ink on Cloth: A detailed exploration of traditional paño art, showcasing inmate expressions through intricate ink work on cloth.

Herencia Azteca: Aztec Art: A tribute to Aztec heritage through detailed inmate artwork, co-created by Eric "Superman" Sturgess and Isaac "Downer" Morquecho.

Top 100 Prison Art Paños: This collection features 100 of the most stunning and culturally significant prison paños, highlighting the intricate artistry of incarcerated individuals. Each piece captures personal stories, cultural heritage, and the emotional depth of life behind bars.

Top 50 Prison Art Paños: Showcasing 50 remarkable prison paños, this book delves into the creative expressions of inmates through powerful imagery and symbolism. It serves as a testament to the resilience and artistic brilliance found within the prison system.

Top 50 Prison Art Paños Of All Time: This curated selection presents the most iconic and timeless prison paños, celebrating the talent and dedication of their creators. Each artwork reveals a unique narrative of hope, faith, and cultural identity from behind the walls.

Made in the USA
Monee, IL
02 November 2026

67378702R00057